SpringerBriefs in Population Studies

More information about this series at http://www.springer.com/series/10047

Zakir Husain · Mousumi Dutta

Fertility Control in a Risk Society

Analysing Contraception Choice of Urban Elites in India

Springer

Zakir Husain
Humanities and Social Sciences
Indian Institute of Technology Kharagpur
Kharagpur, West Bengal
India

Mousumi Dutta
Department of Economics
Presidency University
Kolkata, West Bengal
India

ISSN 2211-3215 ISSN 2211-3223 (electronic)
SpringerBriefs in Population Studies
ISBN 978-81-322-3683-2 ISBN 978-81-322-3685-6 (eBook)
DOI 10.1007/978-81-322-3685-6

Library of Congress Control Number: 2016954592

Printed on acid-free paper

This Springer imprint is published by Springer Nature
The registered company is Springer (India) Pvt. Ltd.
The registered company address is: 7th Floor, Vijaya Building, 17 Barakhamba Road, New Delhi 110 001, India

To our mothers

Acknowledgements

The study was made possible by a financial grant from the Indian Council of Social Science Research (ICSSR), New Delhi, to Dr. Mousumi Dutta. We are grateful to ICSSR for this financial assistance.

We are also grateful to Dr. Saswata Ghosh, Institute of Development Studies, Kolkata, for his help in analysing the National Family Health Survey data, constructing the Standard of Living Indices and overall comments and suggestions. His assistance in writing the paper for *Asian Population Studies* (Zakir Husain, Saswata Ghosh & Mousumi Dutta, 2013, 'Ultramodern Contraception' Re-Examined, *Asian Population Studies*, 9:3, 280–300, DOI: 10.1080/17441730.2013.816480, http://dx.doi.org/10.1080/17441730.2013.816480), which formed the basis for Chap. 3, was invaluable. Permission to use this paper was kindly granted by Routledge and Dr. Saswata Ghosh. We are also grateful to Prof. T.K. Roy and Prof. P.M. Kulkarni for their comments on an early draft of the paper. Three anonymous reviewers also provided useful comments and suggestions. The paper was presented at the Second Conference of the Asian Population Association held at Bangkok in 2012. We received useful suggestions from Gianpierro Dalla Zuanna, Eleanora Hukin, and H. N. Nguyen. We are grateful to all of them.

Two anonymous reviewers of the manuscript provided many useful comments and suggestions as also did the Springer editor, Shinjini Chatterjee. We would like to record our gratitude to all of them. The Springer team deserves special thanks as they were very patient when we repeatedly broke deadlines. They not only gave us more time without even one reproach, but also provided us with many useful suggestions in improving the readability and outreach of the monograph.

We would like to express our gratitude to the field investigators and respondents of the survey. In particular, the help extended by Mayurakshi Chakrabarty should be mentioned.

Finally, we would like to express our gratitude to our family for bearing with us in the difficult phase of writing when all family matters seem to pale into insignificance and the keyboard becomes our sole life.

Any remaining errors remain our responsibility.

Zakir Husain
Mousumi Dutta

About the Book

This book analyses the reasons for relying on behavioural contraception methods among urban 'elites' in India and examines their efficacy in controlling fertility. It also traces variations in contraception choice over the reproductive cycle of women.

Although researchers and policy makers generally equate reliance on behavioural contraceptive methods with low levels of education and awareness and lack of desire to control fertility, this perception has been questioned in recent years. The authors' analysis of the first three rounds of the National Family Health Survey (NFHS) data in India reveals that behavioural contraceptive methods are popular in eastern India. Moreover, it is urban educated women who rely on behavioural methods, and are apparently able to regulate fertility quite effectively with such methods. NFHS data, however, has some limitations and this motivates the authors to explore birth control methods through primary surveys of currently married graduate women in Kolkata.

The use of behavioural contraception methods is a little researched area globally and this is the first book focusing on the topic in India.

Contents

About the Authors

Zakir Husain is an Associate Professor at the Department of Humanities and Social Sciences, Indian Institute of Technology Kharagpur, India. He uses econometric tools and methods to study issues in education, demography, health, gender, and social exclusion. He also teaches general equilibrium analysis, game theory, and econometrics. E-mail: dzhusain@gmail.com

Mousumi Dutta is a Professor at the Department of Economics, Presidency University, Kolkata, India. Her research interests are reproductive health, health economics, gender issues, and built heritage. She teaches applied econometrics and microeconomics. E-mail: dmousumi1970@gmail.com

List of Figures

List of Tables

Chapter 1
Behavioural Contraception Methods

An Introduction

Abstract This chapter starts with a critical look at the traditional literature on behavioural contraception methods. This approach argues that behavioural methods are unreliable and used mainly by uneducated women from low-income households, or by women belonging to religions prohibiting the use of family planning methods. This does not, however, tally with the historical evidence on demographic transition in Europe, nor with the current behavioural patterns in South and South-east Asian countries. In India, too, reliance on behavioural methods is higher than what is expected. Moreover, it is the urban educated and affluent sections of the population who rely on behavioural methods. We suggest three possible explanations for the reliance of urban educated women on behavioural methods. The first approach argues that the use of such methods is a new form of femininity, manifesting itself as a cultural dissent against Western science and technology. The second explanation suggests that it is unsatisfied son preference that explains the reliance on behavioural methods. Finally, we put forward the hypothesis that the stresses and uncertainties of residing in a risk society determine the frequency of sexual intercourse and the conditions in which it takes place. These conditions determine the choice of contraception and why urban educated women rely on behavioural methods.

Keywords Behavioural contraception methods · *Coitus interruptus* · Demographic transition · Rhythm method · Risk society · Son preference · Ultra-modern contraception

1.1 Birth Control Practices

Family planning, or contraceptive, methods are devices used to prevent pregnancy. Some of these methods also protect the user from sexually transmitted devices such as HIV/AIDS and sexually transmitted diseases (STDs). Contraceptive methods may be divided into three major groups. *Folkloric methods* consist of locally described or spiritual methods believed popularly to reduce fertility, but of

Z. Husain and M. Dutta, *Fertility Control in a Risk Society*,
SpringerBriefs in Population Studies, DOI 10.1007/978-81-322-3685-6_1

unproven effectiveness. Such methods consist of herbs, amulets, gris-gris, etc. *Traditional methods* consist of fertility-preventing methods of proven effectiveness, such as rhythm (or calendar) and withdrawal (*coitus interruptus*) methods. These methods are also referred to as behavioural or natural methods. We will use, in general, the term behavioural methods to refer to them. Finally, *modern contraceptive methods* include hormonal methods (i.e. the pill, injectables, and implants), intrauterine devices (IUDs), male and female sterilization, condoms, and invasive vaginal methods (e.g. the diaphragm and spermicides).

1.2 Behavioural Contraception—Better Than Only no Method?

Behavioural methods have been used in many cultures throughout the world since centuries. Even now, data (Table 1.1) show that there are a fairly large proportion of couples practising such methods. It is therefore surprising that the importance of behavioural methods in controlling fertility has traditionally been downplayed in the literature on reproductive health. The literature on family planning considers behavioural contraceptives to be “ineffective”[1] or “unreliable” methods of family planning (Oddens 1997; Zachariah et al. 1994). DeGraff and de Silva (1991, 1996) question whether behavioural methods should be considered as a means of birth control, arguing that users of such methods should be considered to have an unmet demand for contraception. In this vein, the Alan Guttmacher Institute counts women using a traditional method among those “in need of contraception” (Alan Guttmacher Institute 1994: 6). Nguyen and Miller (2012) argue that “The high proportion of couples using traditional methods means that many couples who would like to plan their families are not using the most effective methods to do so and are likely to have unwanted children”.

Bissell (2003) argued that negative medical towards withdrawal as a form of birth control emerged in Western societies in the late nineteenth and early twentieth centuries.

> Physicians viewed the practice of withdrawal as harmful to both men and women. Withdrawal was said to compromise men’s sexual pleasure, which in turn could lead to psychological and physiological distress for both partners. Birth control pioneer Marie Stopes warned that men “could be lured into dangerous overindulgence by the simplicity of withdrawal” (cited in Mclaren 1999: 72). Freud wrote that men who practised withdrawal could “fall ill with anxiety” (cited in Rogow and Horowitz 1995: 149). As recently as the early 1970s, medical literature contained references to withdrawal causing prostate disease, male impotence and female frigidity. However, there is no scientific evidence to back any of these claims. Some current family planning literature still refers to sexual frustration as a problem associated with withdrawal (Bissell 2003).

[1]Although behavioural contraceptives are theoretically effective, in reality their success will depend upon the skill and knowledge of the users (Santow 1993).

Table 1.1 Prevalence of contraceptive methods by types in different countries

Countries	Modern	Rhythm	Withdrawal	Other	Behavioural Total	Ratio (behavioural/behavioural + modern)
Bosnia and Herzegovina	15.7	4.1	26.9	0.7	31.7	66.9
Lebanon	37.0	24.0	24.0	24.0	72.0	66.1
Armenia	22.3	4.8	31.9	1.5	38.2	63.1
Poland	19.0	19.3	11.1	0.0	30.4	61.5
Slovakia	41.0	32.0	32.0	1.0	65.0	61.3
Yemen	9.8	1.1	1.7	8.2	11.0	52.9
Bahrain	30.6	3.2	26.3	1.7	31.2	50.5
Iran	56.0	16.9	16.9	16.9	50.7	47.5
Malaysia	29.8	8.8	6.9	8.9	24.6	45.2
Ukraine	37.6	10.4	19.5	0.0	29.9	44.3
Serbia and Montenegro	32.8	14.2	11.3	0.0	25.5	43.7
Turkey	37.7	1.1	24.4	0.6	26.1	40.9
Italy	38.9	3.6	17.5	0.3	21.4	35.5
Lithuania	30.5	9.3	6.0	0.7	16.0	34.4
Philippines	33.4	6.7	8.2	0.6	15.5	31.7
Syrian Arab Republic	28.3	6.7	1.0	3.6	11.3	28.5
Peru	50.4	14.4	3.2	0.9	18.5	26.9
Pakistan	20.2	1.6	5.3	0.5	7.4	26.8
Jordan	41.2	5.2	9.3	0.1	14.6	26.2
Qatar	32.3	2.3	6.8	1.8	10.9	25.2
Afghanistan	3.6	0.4	0.5	0.3	1.2	25.0
Iraq	10.4	2.1	1.1	0.2	3.4	24.6
Oman	18.2	1.0	2.3	2.3	5.6	23.5

(continued)

Table 1.1 (continued)

Countries	Modern	Rhythm	Withdrawal	Other	Behavioural Total	Ratio (behavioural/ behavioural + modern)
Kazakhstan	52.7	4.7	2.9	5.9	13.5	20.4
Slovenia	59.1	7.0	7.5	0.2	14.7	19.9
Tajikistan	27.3	2.5	3.0	1.1	6.6	19.5
Kuwait	40.9	4.3	3.4	1.6	9.3	18.5
Bangladesh	47.3	6.5	3.6	0.6	10.7	18.4
Latvia	39.3	5.0	3.2	0.5	8.7	18.1
Kyrgyzstan	48.9	3.2	6.0	1.5	10.7	18.0
Spain	67.4	1.9	11.4	0.3	13.6	16.8
Paraguay	60.5	7.7	4.5	0.0	12.2	16.8
United Arab Emirates	23.6	1.6	1.4	0.9	3.9	14.2
Turkmenistan	53.1	2.1	5.3	1.3	8.7	14.1

Source http://www.un.org/esa/population/publications/contraceptive2005/WCU2005.htm, accessed on 15 September 2013

Studies also question the effectiveness of withdrawal, mistakenly arguing that the pre-ejaculate fluid can cause pregnancy (Masters and Johnson 1966; Sjovall 1970; Chng 1983; Kulig 1989). Lack of control of the male partner and inability to identify safe periods are other reasons for the failure of behavioural methods.

> Since traditional methods are less reliable, on average, than modern methods and produce more unwanted births (although traditional methods prevent pregnancies better than does non-use), programs tend to promote modern methods. Researchers have estimated that during typical use, pregnancy rates (based on 12 months of use) for withdrawal and rhythm are 19 and 20 %, respectively, while those for the pill and the Copper-T IUD are 3 and 1 %, respectively (Hubacher et al. 1996).

The high prevalence of behavioural means in many societies has been dismissed offhand as the product of religious taboos on birth control (Ntozi and Kabera 1991; Sharma and Pasha 2011), lack of knowledge about birth control means (Hubacher et al. 1996), and limited access to public health facilities (Hubacher et al. 1996). Users of behavioural forms of birth control are believed to be those least motivated to actually control their fertility or those least able to access more efficient forms of birth control (DeGraff and de Silva 1991, 1996) due to lack of awareness, religious prohibitions, social taboos, etc. It is not surprising therefore that the use of traditional means of contraception has been equated with less educated couples, rural residents, and the inexperienced (Goldberg and Toros 1994; Nguyen and Miller 2012). A popular belief, common even among researchers, is that the persistence of behavioural methods may be explained by their popularity among Roman Catholics and Muslims (Sharma and Pasha 2012), who are not allowed by their religion to adopt modern birth control methods. WHO data (Table 1.1) reveal that the use of behavioural contraceptive methods is comparatively high in countries with a high proportion of Muslims (like Malaysia 24.6 %, Kazakhstan 13.5 %, Iran 16.9 %, West Asian countries 18.1 %) and Roman Catholics (like Philippines 15.5 %, Italy 21.4 %, Spain 13.6 %, Poland 30.4 %, Peru 18.5 %).

Not surprisingly, this has led policy makers and activists to focus on modern methods of birth control in family planning programmes. In Greece, for instance, promotion of modern family planning methods is viewed as means of liberating women from the influence of traditional cultural forces (Paxson 2002). Withdrawal is criticized as being a male-centric birth control method that reinforces patriarchal norms identifying men as active participants and women as passive recipients of sexual activity (du Boulay 1986). Feminists consider withdrawal as "the archaic tool of a macho, phallocratic, and non-permissive society" (Aries 1980: 648).

1.3 Behavioural Contraception and Regulation of Fertility

The reality, however, is quite different. Critics of behavioural contraceptive methods have overlooked the major role played by withdrawal in the demographic transition in Europe. It has remained one of the main methods to regulate fertility in countries

in Italy. The common perception that in developing countries, behavioural methods are used mainly by uneducated women from poor families in rural areas has been proved wrong. Recent studies have showed that behavioural methods are popular among urban educated well-off women (Basu 2005; Gray et al. 1997; Hukin 2012; Kovavisarach and Saringcarnan 2010; Malhotra and Thapa 1990; Nguyen and Miller 2012). It has also been pointed out that failure rates of behavioural methods are not significantly higher than some of the so-called modern methods, believed to be infallible. These researchers posit a role for behavioural methods as an important component of the vector of family planning methods in specific cultures and contexts. Studies have also pointed out that the use of withdrawal for a short period during the lifetime span of sexual relations may also play an important role in curbing fertility among adolescents. For instance, in some countries, withdrawal is often practised by adolescent couples early in their sexual relationship. In urbanizing societies, withdrawal sometimes serves as "a stepping stone to contraceptive use" and "a first step to contraception" (Bulut et al. 1986: 51).

In the following subsections, we examine these findings in greater detail.

1.3.1 Historical Role in Europe

The first demographic transition occurred in Europe, with a substantial decline in fertility from the start of the nineteenth century. Between 1890 and 1920, marital fertility began to decline in most European provinces, with a median decline of about 40 % from 1870 to 1930 (Coale and Treadway 1986: 44). There is a controversy regarding the reasons underlying the decline in marital fertility—"(t)he reduction in fertility accompanying modernisation poses a scientific puzzle that has yet to be solved" (Kaplan et al. 1995: 326). However, there is a general agreement on the *means* of attaining this decline. Historical demographers have pointed out, while delayed nuptiality, abstinence and prolonged breastfeeding were important factors underlying the demographic transition, it was primarily through withdrawal and induced abortions that the reduction in fertility was attained (Wrigley 1969; Lee 2003).

Now, the reduction in fertility in Europe over the course of the nineteenth and twentieth centuries was facilitated by a widespread reliance on withdrawal and, to a lesser extent, induced abortion (e.g. Santow 1993, 1995; Schneider and Schneider 1991, 1996; Dalla Zuanna et al. 2005). But, in the period from 1960 onwards, when fertility began to fall even further, the previously rather homogeneous pattern of contraceptive practice across countries began to diverge. In countries such as Italy, Greece, Spain, and Portugal, the extremely low fertility rates were accompanied with resistance to the diffusion of the pill, IUD, and sterilization for contraceptive purposes (Schneider and Schneider 1996; Dalla Zuanna et al. 2005). Santow (1993: 784) states that "Southern Europe's extraordinary recent fertility decline has been greatly assisted, or even enabled, by withdrawal, despite the availability of modern methods".

Even after the advent of male condoms, a high proportion of women in North Europe have reported using behavioural methods. Around 30 % of British women married between 1930 and 1960 have reported that they had ever used withdrawal (Rowntree and Pierce 1961; Pierce and Rowntree 1961). A slightly later survey, conducted in 1967–68 when fertility had begun to decline from its peak after World War II, found that one in five women was still relying on the behavioural method (Langford 1974). In Sweden, in 1961, one-third of married women had used withdrawal (Gille 1971). About 30 % of respondents in a survey of French women reported reliance on withdrawal (Collomb and Zucker 1977).

Although condoms have replaced behavioural methods subsequently, American studies conducted during the 1930s reported that 20–30 % users had used withdrawal (Riley and White 1940). A survey of Melbourne women, undertaken in 1971, found that 24 % had ever used withdrawal (Caldwell and Ware 1973) and that 13 % of women aged 15–44 were current users (Caldwell et al. 1987).

In South European countries, studies undertaken in countries such as Greece (Symeonidou 1990) and Italy (Castiglioni et al. 2001; Dalla Zuanna et al. 2005) reported that reliance on withdrawal has remained persistently high. Studies of contraception rate in Italy report that about 69–80 % of currently married women rely on withdrawal, while 16–23 % practise the rhythm method (Dalla Zuanna et al. 2005). The case of Italy, a country where fertility has been very low (below 1.5) despite the widespread use of behavioural methods, deserves special attention.

1.3.2 *The Case of Italy*

In Italy, behavioural methods, particularly withdrawal, have been traditionally practised by couples. One reason for this may be religious. In Italy, the Church has traditionally accepted withdrawal as a permissible means of contraception. Flandrin (1988; cited in Dalla Zuanna et al. 2005: 37) has argued that the Church turned a blind eye towards the use of withdrawal, avoiding questioning women about such issues during confession. The indulgence of the Church towards withdrawal, as opposed to their active opposition against modern methods, delayed the transition of Italian society towards condoms and pills. Medical reasons may have also prevented the spread of modern methods (Dalla Zuanna et al. 2005). The distrust of pills by Italian doctors (Fabris and Davis 1978) led them to overemphasize the side effects of pills.

The spread of modern methods, along with the lifting of bans on their advertisements in the 1970s, reduced reliance on behavioural methods, but not eliminated their use:

> Although the use of technological methods has recently started to rise within younger cohorts (especially single women), among Italian women in union there remains a clear delay compared to Northern Europe, and a reluctance to abandon non-technological methods such as withdrawal and natural methods (Gribaldo et al. 2009: 551)

After the 1960s, researchers have observed the trend being sexually active without cohabiting with their partners among Italian couples. Women indulging in such relationships rely on modern contraception such as pills and IUDs. In contrast, reproductive behaviour among women in marital relationships has been slower to change. In particular, the reliance on behavioural methods is still remarkably high:

> "In 1979, 67 % of such women used either withdrawal (58 %) or natural methods (9 %) as their main form of contraception. By 1996, the proportion remained at least 40 % (34 % using withdrawal and 6 % natural methods; Dalla Zuanna et al. 2005). As women in Italy reached some of the lowest fertility rates ever recorded, they used modern methods at a far lower rate than in other European countries. According to the United Nations (2003), only 39 % of Italian women in a union were using modern methods in 1996, compared to 69 % in France in 1994, 72 % in Germany in 1992, and 72 % in Denmark in 1988" (Gribaldo et al. 2009: 556).

1.3.3 Contraception in India

In India, one of the first developing countries to introduce family planning policies, there have been many twists and turns in the policy. However, the thrust on encouraging use of modern methods, particularly among the socio-economically vulnerable sections of the population, has remained a persistent feature of the target-oriented, clinic-centred family planning policy in India (Visaria and Chari 1998; Dyson 2004; Santhya 2003; Vicziany 1982; Srinivasan 1998; Visaria 2000). This has had an impact on the usage pattern of contraceptive methods in the country. The third round of the National Family Health Survey (NFHS-3) reveals that 56 % of currently married women use contraceptives, with 49 % relying on modern methods. Among illiterate women, the latter proportion is 46 %, while a third of women belonging to the lowest wealth index quintile use modern methods. Data presented by Family Planning 2020 (http://www.familyplanning2020.org/entities accessed on 5 January 2016) show that sterilization accounts for about 74 % of the modern contraceptive methods used in India. Further, the use of behavioural methods is low, accounting for just about 8 % of current contraceptive use (International Institute for Population Sciences (IIPS) and Macro International 2007).

On the other hand, National Family Health Survey (NFHS) data indicate that a fairly high proportion of women use behavioural contraceptive methods. In 2005–06, one out of every five women had used such methods at some point of time, with marginal differences between rural and urban areas. The incidence of current use is 8.1 % (urban areas) and 7.6 % (rural areas). Further, the use of such methods has shown a tendency to increase persistently—in the case of rhythm, the proportion of users has risen from 2.7 % (1992–93) to 4.9 % (2005–06), while in the case of withdrawal, the increase is from 1.5 % (1992–93) to 2.5 % (2005–06). Regional analysis reveals that in certain states of East and North-eastern India, reliance on behavioural methods has remained exceptionally high. The last round of NFHS estimates that about 21 % of currently married women in West Bengal rely on behavioural methods; the proportion of users of such methods is also high in Assam (30 %), Manipur (25 %), and Tripura (21 %).

Again, in contrast to the popular views, behavioural methods are popular—not among lowly educated women or those from poor households—but among women with more than 12 years of education (11.8 %) and among women from the top wealth index quintile (9.5 %). This has also been pointed out by other researchers. Basu (2005) points out that among the educated affluent sections of the population —particularly among the residents of urban areas—cultural reorientation may lead to a shift from reliance from modern to behavioural contraceptive methods. Given the socio-economic profile of this user group, behavioural methods are used with both skill and knowledge to control fertility effectively. Given the effectiveness with which such methods are used by the urban elite, Basu coins the term "ultra-modern contraception" to refer to such practices.

1.3.4 Behavioural Methods in South and South-East Asian Countries

Caldwell et al. (1987) and Malhotra and Thapa (1990) argue that traditional methods (primarily rhythm) are used effectively in Sri Lanka. In contrast to the common perception that traditional methods are used primarily by the least knowledgeable and sophisticated members of society, traditional methods are more commonly used in Sri Lanka by the highly educated and reliance on them is just as high among urban women as among rural women. Furthermore, knowledge about the "safe period" is relatively widespread and accurate, and the use of an alternative method during the "unsafe period" is common.

The popularity of behavioural methods has also been reported in South-east Asian countries. A recent study of women aged 15–44 in Thailand found that 70 % had used withdrawal; further, this practice was more popular among the educated respondents and those residing in urban areas (Kovavisarach and Saringcarnan 2010).

Similar trends have been reported in other countries of the region:

> there remain a large number of couples in Vietnam who still rely on these methods, particularly withdrawal and periodic abstinence, for preventing pregnancy. The local term for periodic abstinence is approximately "calculation of safe period"; little is known about exactly how it is practiced, or the knowledge of couples about fertility during the menstrual cycle. According to the Vietnam Population Change and Family Planning Survey in 2008, 10.7 % of couples were using traditional methods. Taken together, traditional methods were the second most common choice for contraception from 2002 to 2008 with more than 13 % of contraceptive use, only after IUD (Nguyen and Miller 2012).

In her doctoral dissertation, Hukin (2012) reports a high reliance on behavioural methods in Cambodia in recent years. Further, the use of behavioural methods was commonly found among the wealthier and educated women who were better able to detect the signs of failure and take appropriate remedial action. In contrast, poor women were financially unable to cope with the costs of abortion and had to rely on modern methods. Fear of side effects, stemming from both contraceptive experiences and notions of health and the body, was found to be the greatest obstacle to the use of modern contraceptives.

The use of traditional methods by currently married women aged 15–49 in the Philippines was also reported to have increased from 15 % in 1993 to 20 % in 1998 (Juarez et al. 2009). An increase in the use of traditional contraceptive methods is observed all the regions, but it is more striking and unexpected that this increase has occurred in Metro Manila, the most urbanized area of the country.

In Bangladesh, 16 % of currently married women were found to rely solely on behavioural methods; if combinations of coitus-dependent methods are considered, this figure is even higher (Gray et al. 1997). Further, "people with higher levels of education, and higher economic status, are significantly more likely to use 'traditional' methods, than people with lower education or economic status" (Gray et al. 1997: 1).

1.3.5 Why the Use of Behavioural Methods Is Under-Reported?

The above discussion shows that the use of behavioural methods has been downplayed in the demographic literature. In fact, some researchers suggest that the actual incidence of withdrawal may be larger than what is reported (Jones et al. 2009; Rogow and Horowitz 1995). There are several reasons why the use of withdrawal may be underestimated, particularly in large studies. Santow (1993) and Jones et al. (2009) point out that most women do not consider behavioural methods to be contraception methods at all. Thus, when asked about birth control methods, they fail to report withdrawal or rhythm.

> … when women are asked about the contraceptive measures they have tried they invariably think only of mechanical or chemical appliances, and never include coitus interruptus…. But when we specifically referred to withdrawal, we almost invariably got the reply, "Oh, yes, he's always been careful" (Florence 1930: 20).

A Demographic Health Survey (DHS) for Pakistan found that a substantially lower proportion of respondents spontaneously reported knowledge about behavioural contraception, relative to prompted response (Rogow and Horowitz 1995). According to Rogow and Horowitz (1995), there are several reasons for this behaviour:

(a) Belief in the ineffectiveness of behavioural methods of birth control;
(b) Distrust of non-technological means of birth control;
(c) Attempt of policy makers to promote modern methods; and
(d) Focus on female-controlled methods that prevent both pregnancy and STD.

Secondly, methodological issues relating to the survey and its administration may lead to underestimation of reliance on behavioural methods. For instance, most of the large-scale studies target currently married women, while one of the main

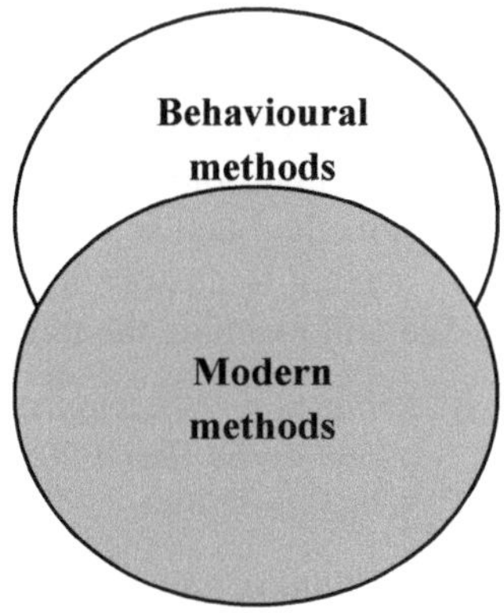

Fig. 1.1 The use of combination and underestimation of reliance on behavioural methods

users of behavioural methods are single young women (Mosher and Christine 1987; Lethbridge 1991; Persson and Jarlbro 1992).

Another problem is that large-scale surveys often require respondents to identify *one* method. The DHS, for instance, requires the respondent to identify whether they are currently using any one of the given methods. This overlooks the fact that couples may use one or more methods in combination. A Costa Rican study found that nine per cent of contraceptive users used a combination of methods, with 41 % of these women using withdrawal (Becker and Sosa 1992). Gray et al.'s study of contraception use in Bangladesh observed that "coitus-dependent methods (condom, withdrawal and rhythm) are used in combination so frequently in Bangladesh that there, at least, calling them distinct methods is misleading" (Gray et al. 1997: 44).

Even when surveys require respondents to identify several methods being used, modern methods are generally entered in the questionnaire:

> In large surveys such as the National Survey of Family Growth (NSFG), when respondents report use of both withdrawal and another more effective method during the same time period, researchers generally categorize the woman as using the more effective method which can lead researchers to underestimate withdrawal use even when it is reported (Jones et al. 2009).

The problem may be depicted in terms of Fig. 1.1. Although all persons within the white circle should be treated as users of behavioural methods, those in the intersection of the grey and white circles (using a combination of modern and behavioural methods) are clubbed with those exclusively in the grey circle and classified as users of only modern methods.

1.4 Why Do People Rely on Behavioural Methods: Alternative Explanations

The reality about popularity of behavioural method and the profile of users, therefore, is quite different from what is commonly believed or what is commonly portrayed in the literature on family planning. The proportion of women using such methods is not negligible; further, the socio-economic background of the users indicates that such use is likely to be a well-informed choice and not the result of either religious taboos or prohibitions, or the result of lack of awareness. This then raises the question: Why do educated women from urban areas rely on a birth control method that is supposedly neither scientific nor reliable? The present study is an attempt to answer this question.

We will examine the three possible solutions to this paradox:

(a) *Reliance on behavioural methods as an expression of modernity and new form of femininity* (Basu 2005; Johnson-Hanks 2002; Krause 2005; Schneider and Schneider 1996):

Basu (2005) argues that reliance on behavioural methods to regulate fertility reflects a new form of femininity as it is an expression of cultural dissent against Western science.

She argues that poor and uneducated women view the body as a functional unit to be used for basic sociocultural and economic tasks subject to interference from menstruation and pregnancies. So, once the desired family size is attained, the two processes are viewed as undesirable. This attitude encourages interest in modern contraceptive methods that can be easily used.

The demand for behavioural contraception methods emerges as a reaction to such misplaced modernism, through the emergence of postmodern attitudes among urban educated women. Instead of viewing the body as a functional producer unit, it is increasingly viewed as a consumer unit, shifting the focus from ritual purity of the body to personal hygiene. This growing "body consciousness" among the urban elite encourages urban educated "ultra-modern" women to avoid modern contraceptive methods associated with Western science and technology and adopt family control methods that are natural, less invasive, and in tune with emerging forms of femininity—and linked with tradition and the past. In keeping with the ultra-modern attitude of the users, behavioural methods have been referred to as ultra-modern contraception (Basu 2005).

(b) *Reliance on behavioural methods at moments of ambiguity about optimal family size to satisfy son preference* (Husain et al. 2013):

This approach starts by pointing out that contraceptive choice is conceptualized in the literature on fertility control in static terms. An analysis of the motives underlying contraception choice should take into account that objectives of intercourse and the desire to reproduce vary with gender parity and stage of the life cycle. This will influence the choice of contraceptive combination at any point of time. While the literature commonly models the relationship between fertility and contraception choice as in Fig. 1.2a, b, in reality, there is an interaction between the two, so that the actual situation resembles Fig. 1.2c.

The essence of our argument is that contraception choice is not constant but may change over time.

Researchers do not consider the possibility that preferences may shift over different phases of the reproductive life cycle. In particular, the studies on

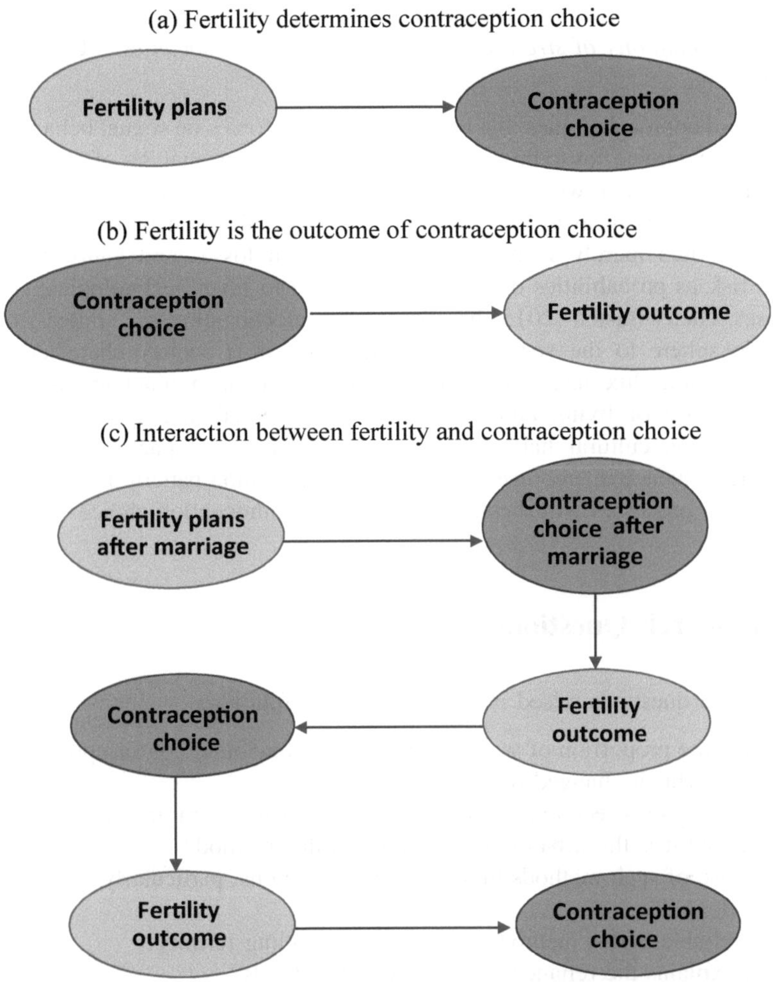

Fig. 1.2 Modelling relationship between fertility and contraception choice

ultra-modern contraception do not consider the possibility that women may adopt modern methods during their peak reproductive years and switch to periodic abstinence afterwards. Such studies also overlook ethnographic evidence showing that couples may use behavioural methods as a transitory method when they are ambivalent about pregnancy (Gribaldo et al. 2009) or undecided about its timing (Fisher 2000). Given that son preference has been known to guide fertility preferences in India, it is quite possible that users who have unsatisfied fertility desires, particularly for sons, use behavioural practices as a transitory method. This would explain why behavioural methods are used by the urban elite—as it is among such families that son preference and sex selection are prominently displayed (Jha et al. 2011; Nanda and Véron 2005).

(c) *Reliance on behavioural methods as an optimal method of fertility control under conditions of stress and uncertainty in "risk societies"* (Gietel-Basten 2015):

The third approach argues that influence of social forces on sexual behaviour and contraception choice has to be explicitly considered in any analysis of contraception choice. In this context, we rely on the concept of risk society (Giddens 1990, 1991; Beck 1992). Moving away from a neutral conceptualization of risk as a neutral term, concerned merely with probabilities or with losses and gains, Beck had defined risk as probabilities of physical harm due to given technological or other processes. Gietel-Basten (2015) has argued that globalization has spilled from the economic sphere to the social domain, resulting in a society characterized by constant tension, flux, and change. The resultant dynamism generates risks related to the standard of living and welfare, creating sexual anxiety among males.[2] Simultaneously, cultural habits and (non-)availability of space define sleeping habits and influence intercourse patterns. The cohabitation pattern that emerges out of these two processes will dictate the choice of contraception choice.

1.5 Research Questions

The research questions raised in this study are as follows:

- What is the proportion of women relying on behavioural contraceptive methods in India? Has it changed over time?
- What is the socio-economic profile of users of behavioural methods in India? Is it true that it is the urban elite who rely on this method?
- Is the use of such methods higher in certain regions, particularly in the state of West Bengal?
- How reliable is this method in terms of controlling fertility?
- What explains the reliance on behavioural methods?
- Do couples rely solely on this method? Or do they combine methods? Further, does the method mix vary over the reproductive life cycle of women?

1.6 Data Sources

We have used two data sets in our analysis. The work starts by using NFHS data. This data set is the largest repository of information on reproductive health in India. The survey was undertaken in four years—in 1992–93, 1998–99, 2005–06, and

[2]This is in contrast to premodern societies with primitive medical facilities and technology where the risk is centred around mortality.

2014–15. We have used the first three rounds,[3] merging them into a single data set. This enables us to compare changes in reproductive health behaviour over more than a decade at the national level. The analysis also focuses on data from West Bengal, a state in Eastern India. The choice of West Bengal is guided by the high usage of behavioural methods in the state. Further, in terms of both population and geographical area (total population is 91.3 million, and female population is 44.4 million, according to the 2011 Census; its area is 34,267 sq. miles), West Bengal is larger than many European, Latin American, and Asian countries.

NFHS data, however, have certain limitations discussed in detail in Chap. 2. For instance, it elicits the information on only one contraception method; further, the information obtained is for current use and ever use. The information provided in NFHS, therefore, is incomplete and does not provide information to analyse issues such as transition of contraception choice and reliance on the combination of contraception methods. The failure of NFHS data to incorporate these aspects led us to supplement the initial analysis with data from a primary survey undertaken in Kolkata. The choice of the survey site is dictated by the finding that reliance on behavioural methods is high in Eastern India, particularly in West Bengal, and in urban areas. The survey covered currently married graduate women at risk (i.e. non-pregnant women who are not sterile).

1.7 Scheme of Study

The remaining part of the study is structured as follows. Chap. 3 describes the database, sample profile, and statistical methods employed. Findings are stated and discussed in the next three chapters. In Chap. 3, we summarize the concept of "ultra-modern contraception" and the cultural explanation offered to explain the reliance on behavioural methods by urban elite women based on Basu (2005). This discussion is followed by an analysis of the shortcomings of this explanation using NFHS data. The results of the primary survey are discussed in Chaps. 4–6. Chap. 4 re-examines the hypothesis that son preference and ambiguity about family size and composition are the motivating forces underlying the choice of behavioural methods. In Chap. 5, we shift from what we call the static approach to contraception methods. While this view focuses on the current use of a single method, a more complete approach is to study the transition of combination of contraception method over the reproductive life cycle of women. The study shows how transition matrices may be used to examine such shifts. The analysis shows that there is a little evidence in support of son preference. Rather, as discussed in Chap. 7, the emerging analysis of behaviour in risk societies can provide an explanation of why the urban elite rely on behavioural methods. A concluding chapter sums up the main findings and identifies the possible avenues for further research in this area.

[3]The fourth-round unit-level data are not available at the time of preparing the manuscript.

References

Alan Guttmacher Institute. (1994). Women and reproductive health in sub-Saharan Africa. Washington, DC: Alan Guttmacher Institute.

Aries, P. (1980). Two successive motivations for the declining birth rate in the West. *Population and Development Review, 6*, 645–665.

Basu, A. M. (2005). Ultramodern contraception: Social class and family planning in India. *Asian Population Studies, 1*(3), 303–323.

Becker, S., & Sosa, D. (1992). An experiment using a month by-month calendar in a family planning survey in Costa Rica. *Studies in Family Planning, 23*(6), 386–391.

Beck, U. (1992). *Risk society: Towards a new modernity*. London: Sage Publications.

Bissell, M. (2003). Withdrawal: Historical, cultural and current perspectives on its use. *The Canadian Journal of Human Sexuality, 12*, 3–4. http://www.biomedsearch.com/article/Withdrawal-historical-cultural-currentperspectives/120099104.html. Accessed May 20, 2014.

Bulut, A., Cilingiroglu, N., & Bertran, M. (1986). Is withdrawal a handicap for fertility regulation? Nufusbilim Derg. *Turkish Journal of Population Studies, 8*, 45–55.

Caldwell, J. C., & Ware, H. (1973). The evolution of family planning in Australia. *Population Studies, 27*, 7–31.

Caldwell, J., Gaminiratne, K. H., Caldwell, P., de Silva, S., Caldwell, B., Weeraratne, N., et al. (1987). The role of traditional fertility regulation in Sri Lanka. *Studies in Family Planning, 18*(1), 1–21.

Coale, A. J., & Treadway, R. (1986). A summary of the changing distribution of overall fertility, marital fertility and the proportions married in the provinces of Europe. In A. J. Coale & S. Watkins (Eds.), *The decline of fertility in Europe*. Princeton: Princeton University Press.

Castiglioni, M., Dalla Zuanna, G., & Loghi, M. (2001). Planned and Unplanned Births and Conceptions in Italy, 1970–1995. *European Journal of Population, 17*(3), 207–233.

Chng, C. L. (1983). The male role in contraception: Implications for health education. *Journal of School Health, 53*(3), 197–201.

Collomb, P., & Zucker, E. (1977). Aspects culturels et socio-psychologiques de lafe'condite Francaise. Une Enquete de l'INED (1971) Travaux et Documents, Cahier No. 80. Paris, Presses Universitaires de France.

Dalla Zuanna, G., De Rose, A., & Racioppi, F. (2005). Low fertility and limited diffusion of modern contraception in Italy during the second half of the twentieth century. *Journal of Population Research, 22*, 21–48.

DeGraff, D. S., & de Silva, V. (1991). Unmet need for contraception in Sri Lanka. *International Family Planning Perspectives, 17*(4), 123–130.

DeGraff, D. S., & de Silva, V. (1996). A new perspective on the definition and measurement of unmet need for contraception. *International Family Planning Perspectives, 22*(4), 140–147.

du Boulay, J. (1986). Women-images of their nature and destiny in rural Greece. In J. Dubisch (Ed.), *Gender and power in rural Greece*. Princeton: Princeton University Press.

Dyson, T. (2004). India's population—The past. In T. Dyson, R. Cassen, & L. Visaria (Eds.), *Twenty-first century India—Population, economy, human development and the environment*. New Delhi: Oxford University Press.

Fabris, G., & Davis, R. (1978). *Il Mito del Sesso*. Milan: Mondadori.

Fisher, K. (2000). Uncertain aims and tacit negotiation: Birth control practices in Britain 1925–1950. *Population Development Review, 26*, 295–317.

Flandrin, J. L. (1988). *La Chiesa e il Controllo delle Nascite*. Transeuropa: Ancona.

Florence, L. S. (1930). *Birth control on trial*. London: George Allen & Unwin Ltd..

Giddens, A. (1990). *Consequences of modernity*. Cambridge: Polity Press.

Giddens, A. (1991). *Modernity and self-Identity. Self and society in the late modern age*. Stanford: Stanford University Press.

Gietel-Basten, S. (2015). Individualisation, risk society and ultra-low fertility. *Plenary lecture delivered at Third Asian Population Conference*, Kuala Lumpur, 26–30 July.

Gille, H. (1971). Family limitation in Europe. *Paper presented in International Population Conference, London 1969*, (Conference proceedings, Vol. 2, pp. 1277–1293), Liege: International Union for the Scientific Study of Population.

Goldberg, H. I., & Toros, A. (1994). The use of traditional methods of contraception among Turkish couples. *Studies in Family Planning, 25*, 122–128.

Gray, A., Chowdhury, J. H., Caldwell, B., & Al-Sabir, A. (1997). *Traditional family planning in Bangladesh*. Dhaka: Population Council.

Gribaldo, A., Judd, M. D., & Kertzer, D. I. (2009). An imperfect contraceptive society: Fertility and contraception in Italy. *Population Development Review, 35*, 551–584.

Hubacher, D., Suazo, M., Terrell, S., & Pinel, M. (1996). Examining the increasing prevalence of traditional contraceptive methods in Honduras. *International Family Planning Perspectives, 22* (4), 163–168.

Hukin, E. (2012). Contraceptive choice, abortion and socio-economic status, Poster presentation. *Paper presented in Second Asian Population Association Conference*, Bangkok, 26–29 August.

Husain, Z., Ghosh, S., & Dutta, M. (2013). 'Ultramodern contraception' re-examined: Cultural dissent, or son preference. *Asian Population Studies, 9*(3), 280–300.

International Institute for Population Sciences and Macro International. (2007). *National Family Health Survey (NFHS-3), 2005–06: India* (Vol. I). Mumbai: International Institute for Population Sciences.

Jha, P., Kesler, M. A., Kumar, R., Ram, F., Ram, U. L., Aleksandrowicza, L., et al. (2011). Trends in selective abortions of daughters in India: Analysis of nationally representative birth histories from 1990 to 2005 and census data from 1991 to 2011. *Lancet, 377*(781), 1921–1928.

Johnson-Hanks, J. (2002). On the modernity of traditional contraception: Time and the social context of fertility. *Population and Development Review, 28*, 229–241.

Jones, R. K., Fennell, J., Higgins, J. A., & Blanchard, K. (2009). Better than nothing or savvy risk-reduction practice? *The Importance of Withdrawal. Contraception, 79*(6), 407–410.

Juarez, F., Cabigon, J., & Singh, S. (2009). High prevalence of traditional methods and unwanted pregnancies: Barriers to obtaining family planning services in the Philippines. Paper presented in Population Association of America 2009 Annual Meeting, Detroit, Michigan, April 30–May 2. http://paa2009.princeton.edu/download.aspx?submissionId=90756. Accessed July 15, 2011.

Kaplan, H. S., Lancaster, J. B., Bock, J. A., & Johnson, S. E. (1995). Does observed fertility maximize fitness among new Mexican men? A test of an optimality model and a new theory of parental investment in the embodied capital of offspring. *Human Nature, 6*, 325–360.

Kovavisarach, E., & Saringcarnan, P. (2010). Coitus interruptus in female patients seeking services at Obstetrics and Gynecology Department in Rajavithi Hospital. *Journal of Medical Association Thailand, 93*, 1356–1359.

Krause, E. (2005). *A crisis of births: Population politics and family making in Italy*. Belmont, CA: Thomson/Wadsworth.

Kulig, J. W. (1989). Adolescent contraception: Non-hormonal methods. *Pediatric Clinics of North America, 36*(3), 717–726.

Langford, B. J., & Langford, C. J. (1974). Church attendance and self-perceived altruism. *Journal for the Scientific Study of Religion*, 13, 221–222.

Lee, R. (2003). The demographic transition: Three centuries of fundamental change. *Journal of Economic Perspectives, 17*(4), 167–190.

Lethbridge, D. J. (1991). Coitus interruptus: Considerations as a method of birth control. *Journal of Obstetric, Gynecological, & Neonatal Nursing, 20*(1), 80–85.

Malhotra, A., & Thapa, S. (1990). *Determinants of contraceptive method choice in Sri Lanka: An update from a 1987 survey*. Unpublished paper, N.C.: Family Health International, Research Triangle Park.

Masters, W. H., & Johnson, V. E. (1966). *Human sexual response*. Boston MA: Little, Brown and Company.

McLaren, A. (1999). *Twentieth-century sexuality: A history*. Oxford UK: Blackwell Publishers.

Mosher, W. D., & Christine, A. B. (1987). First premarital contraceptive use: United States, 1960–82. *Studies in Family Planning, 18*(2), 83–95.

Nanda, A., & Véron, J. (2005). Child sex ratio imbalances, fertility behaviour and development in India: Recent evidence from Haryana and Punjab. In I. Attańe & J. Véron (Eds.), *Gender discrimination among young children in Asia*. French Institute of Pondicherry: Pondicherry.

Nguyen, H. N., & Miller, P. (2012, August). The use of traditional contraceptive methods in a northern province in Vietnam. *Paper presented in Second Asian Population Conference*, Bangkok, 26–29 August.

Ntozi, J. P. M., & Kabera, J. (1991). Family planning in rural Uganda: Knowledge and use of modern and traditional methods in Ankole. *Studies in Family Planning, 22*, 116–123.

Oddens, B. J. (1997). Determinants of contraceptive use among women of reproductive age in Great Britain and Germany. II: Psychological factors. *Journal of Biosocial Science, 29*, 437–470.

Paxson, H. (2002). Rationalizing sex: Family planning and the making of modern lovers in urban Greece. *American Ethnologist, 29*(2), 307–334.

Persson, E., & Jarlbro, G. (1992). Early sexual initiation is an indicator of hazardous sexual behaviour. *Lakartidningen, 89*(15), 1276–1280.

Pierce, R. M., & Rowntree, G. (1961). Birth control in Britain, Part 2. Contraceptive methods used by couples married in the last thirty years. *Population Studies, 15*, 121–160.

Riley, JW., & White M (1940) Uses of various methods of contraception. *American Sociological review*, 5: 890–903.

Rogow, D., & Horowitz, S. (1995). Withdrawal: A review of the literature and an agenda for research. *Studies in Family Planning, 26*, 140–153.

Rowntree, G., & Pierce, R. M. (1961). Birth control in Britain, Part 1. Attitudes and practices among persons married since the first world war. *Population Studies, 15*, 3–31.

Santhya, K. G. (2003). Changing family planning scenario in India: An overview of recent evidence. *South & East Asia Regional Working Papers no. 17*. New Delhi: Population Council.

Santow, G. (1993). Withdrawal in the twentieth century. *Population Development Review, 19*(4), 767–792.

Santow, G. (1995). Coitus interruptus and the control of natural fertility. *Population Studies, 49*(1), 19–43.

Schneider, J., & Schneider, P. (1991). Sex and respectability in an age of fertility decline: A Sicilian case study. *Social Science and Medicine, 33*(8), 885–895.

Schneider, J., & Schneider, P. (1996). *Festival of the poor: Fertility decline and the ideology of class in Sicily 1860–1980*. Tucson: Arizona Press.

Sharma, S., & Pasha, A. (2011). Are muslim women behind in their knowledge and use of contraception in India? *Journal of Public Health and Epidemiology, 3*(13), 632–641.

Sharma, S., & Pasha, A. (2012). Modern and traditional contraceptive choices for Muslim women in India. *International Journal of Physical and Social Sciences, 2*(6), http://bit.ly/29dBDbF. Accessed July 4, 2016.

Sjovall, E. (1970). Coitus interruptus. In M. S. Calderone (Ed.), *Manual of family planning and contraceptive practice*. Baltimore MD: The Williams and Wilkins Company.

Srinivasan, K. (1998). Population policies and programmes since independence: A saga of great expectations and poor performance. *Demography India, 27*, 1–22.

Symeonidou, H. (1990). *Fertility and employment of women in the greater Athens area*. Athens: National Centre for Social Research.

United Nations. (2003). World contraceptive use 2003. Wall chart. Population division, Department of Economic and Social Affairs.

Vicziany, M. (1982). Coercion in a soft state: The family planning programme of India: Part 1: The myth of voluntarism. *Pacific Affairs, 55*(3), 373–402.

Visaria, P., & Chari, V. (1998). India's population policy and family planning programme: Yesterday, today and tomorrow. In A. Jain (Ed.), *Do population policies matter? Fertility and politics in Egypt, India, Kenya and Mexico*. New York: Population Council.

Visaria, P. (2000). *Population policy in India: Evolution, performance and challenges*. New Delhi: Mimeograph, Institute of Economic Growth.

Wrigley, E. A. (1969). *Population and History*. London: Widenfeld and Nicholson.

Zachariah, K. C., Irudaya Rajan, S., Sharma, P. S., Navanttham, K., Gopinath Nair, P. S., & Mishra, U. S. (1994). *Demographic transition in Kerala in 1990s*. Trivandrum: Centre for Development Studies.

Chapter 2
Methodological Issues

Abstract The chapter describes the data used in the study and the methods employed for collecting and analysing the data. Two sources of data are used. The first part of the analysis is based on unit level data from the three rounds of National Family Health Survey (NFHS). The data, however, has certain limitations; this forces us to explore the issues thrown up by our analysis of NFHS data using data collected through a primary survey of Kolkata, a metropolitan city in eastern India. The survey was undertaken in 2012–13. Details of the sampling frame and sampling method are given. We also describe the socio-demographic profile of both samples—from the NFHS data and from the primary survey. The chapter concludes by identifying the statistical methods used to analyse the data.

Keywords Kolkata · Logit model · Multinomial logit · National family health survey · Sequential logit · Transition matrices

2.1 Introduction

The study is based on two sources of data. One source is secondary—Demographic Health Survey (DHS) data, popularly known as National Family Health Survey (NFHS) data in India. The other source of data is a primary survey undertaken in the metropolitan city of Kolkata. The NFHS data is used to undertake a preliminary examination of the ultramodern hypothesis as stated by Basu (2005). The justification of starting with the NFHS data is that it is a nationally representative data set, covering three years spanning more than a decade. Moreover, it has respondents from different education and income levels and from different states. Thirdly, the original hypothesis was formed based on an analysis of NFHS data.

However, NFHS data has its limitations. These limitations relate to the nature of questions asked about contraceptive choice—namely only current contraceptive choice is elicited. We have argued in this study that fertility preferences of women may change over their reproductive cycle. This implies that choice of contraceptive may change over the life cycle. This is not captured by the NFHS data. Further,

Z. Husain and M. Dutta, *Fertility Control in a Risk Society*,
SpringerBriefs in Population Studies, DOI 10.1007/978-81-322-3685-6_2

studies reveal that women do not always rely on a single method; rather they often tend to combine two or more contraceptive methods. NFHS data, however, asks women to identify only one method. This makes the NFHS data set unsuitable to examine the other two explanations of the reliance on behavioural methods. To overcome these limitations, we have undertaken a primary survey of graduate women in Kolkata. The objective was to supplement the analysis of NFHS data and try to address unanswered questions thrown up during the analysis.

In this chapter, we briefly describe the characteristics of the NFHS data set, the sampling methodology and the profile of the sample. This is succeeded by a discussion of the sampling strategy employed to undertake the primary survey and profile of respondents. In the last section of the chapter, the methodology used to analyse the data is described.

2.2 National Family Health Survey Data

The preliminary part of this analysis is based on three rounds of the NFHS undertaken in India. These surveys are conducted under the stewardship of the Ministry of Health and Family Welfare, Government of India, with the International Institute for Population Sciences, Mumbai, serving as the nodal agency. Information is collected through a household survey which provides estimates of indicators of population, health, and nutrition by background characteristics at the national and state levels. Information was collected based on individual interviews. NFHS forms part of the internationally known DHS series. Four rounds of the survey have been conducted so far—in 1992–1993, 1998–1999, 2005–2006 and 2014–15. The data for the last round is, however, yet to be released. The data collected is placed in five files—women's file, birth file, children's (generally called kid's) file, couple's file and household characteristics file.

The Woman's Questionnaire collected information from all ever-married women age 15–49 who were usual residents of the sample household or visitors who stayed in the sample household the night before the interview. In the first round of the NFHS survey, the age group was slightly larger—women aged between 13 years and 49 years were interviewed. The questionnaire covered the following topics:

- *Background characteristics*: Questions on age, marital status, education, employment status, and place of residence provide information on characteristics likely to influence demographic and health behaviour. Questions are also asked about a woman's husband, gender roles, and the treatment of women in the household.
- *Reproductive behaviour and intentions*: Questions cover dates and survival status of all births, current pregnancy status, and future childbearing intentions of each woman.
- *Quality of care*: Questions assess the quality of family planning and health services.

- *Knowledge and use of contraception*: Questions cover knowledge and use of specific family planning methods. For women not using family planning, questions are included about reasons for non-use and intentions about future use.
- *Sources of family planning*: Questions determine where a user obtained her family planning method.
- *Antenatal, delivery, and postpartum care*: The questionnaire collects information on whether women received antenatal and postpartum care, who attended the delivery, and the nature of complications during pregnancy for recent births.
- *Breastfeeding and health*: Questions cover feeding practices, the length of breastfeeding, immunization coverage, and recent occurrences of diarrhoea, fever, and cough for young children.
- *Reproductive health*: Questions assess various aspects of women's reproductive health and the type of care sought for health problems.
- *Status of women*: The questionnaire asks about women's autonomy and violence against women.
- *Knowledge of AIDS*: Questions assess women's knowledge of AIDS and the sources of their knowledge, as well as knowledge about ways to avoid getting AIDS.

The women, or individual, files contain information about women aged 15–49 years. The information are extracted from the three rounds and merged to form a single dataset. Since the datasets do not match perfectly, in terms of both coding and parameters on which information are provided, merging leads to loss of information. But such loss is offset by the fact that we have information on reproductive behaviour over a period of time, spanning more than a decade (from 1992–1993 to 2005–2006), when economic restructuring of the economy and integration with the global economy was leading to corresponding changes in the social structure. After merging, currently married women, who are not currently

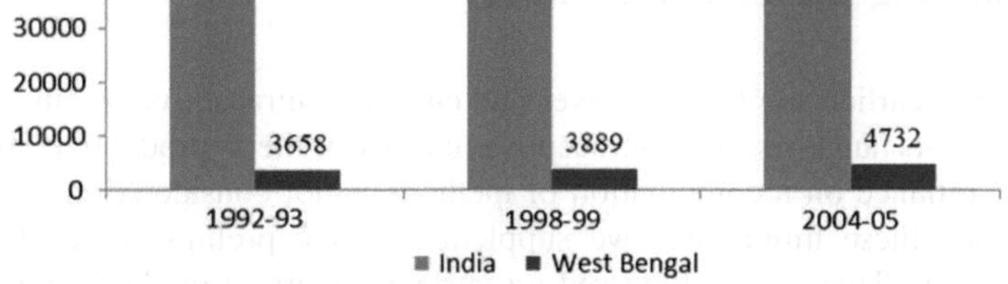

Fig. 2.1 Number of women at risk in each Round. *Note* Women at risk refers to currently married women who are not currently pregnant—India and West Bengal

pregnant, were selected; the remaining respondents were dropped. This results in a sample size of 2,37,822 women at risk, of which 12,279 are from West Bengal. The round-wise sample size is given in Fig. 2.1.

2.3 Profile of NFHS Sample

The sample characteristics of the final sample are briefly reported in Table 2.1. It may be seen that about 35 % (40 % in West Bengal) of the all-India sample reside in urban area. Keeping pace with rapid urbanization, the share of urban population has increased over the three rounds for both the total and Bengal samples. In India, socio-religious identity of respondents has been observed to be a major influence on socio-economic status and behavioural patterns. Hindu Forward Castes (HFCs), consisting of Upper Castes and Other Backward Castes, compose the largest socio-religious group—representing over half of the total sample. Hindu Scheduled Castes (HSC) and Hindu Scheduled Tribes (HSTs) are other groups within Hindus, the major religious group in West Bengal. While the share of HSTs in the sample is quite low, HSCs consists of a larger proportion of the sample, particularly in West Bengal. Muslims comprises the largest religious minority groups, with their share being almost one fourth in West Bengal.

Most of the women belong to the 20–29 and 30–39 year age groups, while the share of women aged below 20 years is quite low. The proportion of illiterate women is highest, followed by those with secondary level education. Over time, the share of illiterates in sample has fallen, while the share of secondary-educated women has increased. A similar pattern is observed with respect to education of respondent partner. While the majority of women are not engaged in economic activities, this share has decreased between the last two rounds. Feminization of agriculture has led to increase in share of women in the primary sector. In comparison partners were concentrated in primary sector in the first round, but have shifted to the tertiary sector in subsequent sectors. The distribution of respondents by standard of living index groups is more or less even across groups, with the 'poorest' group having the highest frequency.

2.4 Planning the Primary Survey

As mentioned earlier, the focus on ever and current contraceptive use in the NFHS survey prevents analysis of contraceptive use over the reproductive life cycle. Moreover, reliance on a combination of methods is not considered in NFHS data. To overcome these limitations, we supplemented the preliminary analysis by a primary survey. This survey focussed on currently married graduate women aged 23–45 years. It was undertaken from November 2012 to August 2013.

Table 2.1 Profile of respondents in India and West Bengal—NFHS Rounds

Socio-economic correlates		India				West Bengal			
		1992–1993	1998–1999	2005–2006	Total	1992–1993	1998–1999	2005–2006	Total
Type of place of residence	Urban	31.2	31.4	44.0	35.7	21.5	44.7	50.1	39.9
	Rural	68.8	68.6	56.0	64.3	78.5	55.3	49.9	60.1
Socio-religious identity[a]	H-SC	10.6	15.2	14.7	13.5	9.1	21.0	22.1	17.9
	H-ST	7.2	7.1	5.9	6.7	4.1	3.7	3.2	3.6
	H-Others	61.0	56.0	54.1	57.0	58.5	54.6	48.8	53.5
	Muslim	10.2	11.7	12.8	11.6	26.3	18.5	24.6	23.2
	Others	11.0	10.0	12.6	11.2	2.0	2.2	1.4	1.8
Grouped age of respondents	13–19 years	8.3	7.0	4.6	6.6	11.3	6.3	6.6	7.9
	20–29 years	37.9	36.8	34.4	36.3	40.0	37.0	34.4	36.9
	30–39 years	32.8	34.4	36.7	34.7	30.3	34.6	34.7	33.3
	40–50 years	21.0	21.8	24.3	22.4	18.3	22.1	24.3	21.8
Highest education of respondent[b]	No education	56.3	49.4	38.9	48.0	52.4	37.2	35.2	41.0
	Primary	14.6	16.9	15.5	15.7	20.4	23.5	19.8	21.1
	Secondary	21.0	24.2	36.7	27.5	21.1	28.4	36.3	29.3
	Higher	8.1	9.5	8.9	8.8	6.0	10.9	8.7	8.6
Occupation of respondent[c]	Unemployed	67.8	65.4	59.6	64.2	78.8	79.2	69.6	75.4
	Primary	19.8	29.3	30.2	26.5	9.7	16.6	19.0	15.5
	Tertiary	12.3	5.2	10.3	9.3	11.5	4.2	11.4	9.1
Highest education of partner	No education	31.0	25.3	22.4	26.2	34.9	23.3	26.3	27.9
	Primary	17.4	18.3	15.3	17.0	21.8	24.1	18.8	21.4
	Secondary	33.7	36.8	47.6	39.6	29.3	32.6	40.0	34.5
	Higher	17.9	19.5	14.7	17.3	14.0	20.0	14.8	16.2

(continued)

Table 2.1 (continued)

Socio-economic correlates		India				West Bengal			
		1992–1993	1998–1999	2005–2006	Total	1992–1993	1998–1999	2005–2006	Total
Occupation of partner	Unemployed	3.8	4.1	2.3	3.4	2.8	6.1	2.1	3.6
	Primary	36.7	66.5	61.4	55.0	46.0	58.9	58.9	55.0
	Tertiary	59.5	29.4	36.3	41.6	51.3	35.0	39.1	41.4
Grouped Standard of Living Index[d]	Poorest	24.4	22.0	25.5	23.8	27.2	24.9	20.6	24.5
	Poor	18.0	20.1	21.1	19.6	18.8	17.7	23.2	19.5
	Middle	19.2	20.0	15.1	18.3	20.5	19.3	22.4	20.5
	Rich	18.1	18.6	20.4	18.9	17.9	22.0	24.1	21.2
	Richest	20.2	19.4	17.9	19.3	15.5	16.1	9.7	14.2

Note

[a]Socio-religious identity is formed by combining information on religion and caste of respondents. The following groups are formed: HSC, Hindu Scheduled Tribes (HST), Hindu-Others, comprising of Forward Castes and Other Backward Castes (H-Others)

[b]Respondents are clubbed by educational levels into four groups: no education (illiterate, below primary), completed primary, completed secondary and higher (including those completing higher secondary levels, graduates, and postgraduates)

[c]Information on occupation of both partner and respondent was recoded to form three classes: Unemployed (including unemployed, household and domestic work, do not know), Primary (agricultural self-employed, agricultural employed, skilled and unskilled) and Tertiary (Professionals, Technical, Managerial, Sales, and Services)

[d]Standard of Living Index was calculated for each of the three rounds following the method suggested in Roy et al. (1999). The SLI scores were used to divide the samples in each round into quintile groups

The first part of the questionnaire collects information on the demographic profile of the respondent—age, marital status, religion, caste, family size, linguistic group, education, etc. This was followed by questions on ownership of assets and expenditure pattern that indicate standard of living in Kolkata. These were subsequently combined to form standard of living indices. The third section elicited information about awareness of contraception methods, use of such methods and reasons underlying choice. In the next section, the focus was on behavioural methods. The respondent was asked whether she used withdrawal or calendar method, reasons for choice, satisfaction with these methods, failure of the methods, etc. The fifth section sought information about degree of empowerment of the respondent. The information was again used to construct an index of empowerment. The final section traced the choice of contraception method over the life cycle, divided into several stages by conceptions.

2.4.1 Sampling Strategy

Respondents were selected from women residing Kolkata. This city is the capital of West Bengal, one of the largest states in eastern India, and is also the third largest metropolitan city in India. Kolkata is the cultural, educational and commercial centre of West Bengal. The choice Kolkata was motivated by the high reliance on behavioural methods in urban West Bengal, as revealed in the NFHS data.

The Kolkata metropolitan area, spread over 1886.67 km^2, comprises 3 municipal corporations, 39 local municipalities and 24 *panchayat samitis*, as of 2011. The total population of this urban agglomeration is 4.5 million persons in 2011. The Kolkata Municipality may be divided into three zones. North Kolkata is the oldest part of the city. Characterized by nineteenth century architecture and narrow alleyways, the culture of this part of the city is comparatively conservative. Central Kolkata hosts the central business district. South Kolkata developed after India gained independence in 1947; it includes upscale neighbourhoods, with inhabitants commonly believed to be more dynamic, liberal and progressive. Two planned townships in the greater Kolkata region are Bidhannagar and Rajarhat (also called Salt Lake City and New Town, respectively). Like South Kolkata, these areas are also supposed to be modern in their outlook and life style. In addition, Kolkata has extensive suburbs.

The information being elicited was of an extremely sensitive nature. The survey was administered by women field investigators who were trained for this purpose and with experience in undertaking reproductive health-related surveys. The Investigators were instructed explain the purpose the survey and to seek the informed consent of respondents before initiating the interview. Further, the respondent could refuse to continue with the interview at any point during the survey.

The choice of the sampling method is a crucial element in any survey-based study. Although a random survey is best as it is amenable to statistical analysis and can be generalized, there are practical limitations to using this method particularly in sensitive surveys like the present one. A common recourse in such cases is to adopt snowball sampling, starting with a respondent and requesting her to refer

Investigators to other possible respondents. This method is popular among sociologists and anthropologists, and often used in qualitative surveys. The problem with this method is that respondents may refer investigators to similar or like-minded persons so that the sample becomes homogenous. We, therefore, adopted a quota-based sampling method. This may be justified as follows.

Our hypothesis that it is the highly educated (graduate and above) women who rely on such contraceptive methods guides the choice of graduate women as respondents. Among graduates, however, we wanted to cover women from different religious and social groups, from different occupations, and residing in different parts of Kolkata. This, along with practical considerations, led us to adopt a quota-based sampling strategy. Although the use of a non-random strategy affects the extent to which the results can be generalized, this sampling strategy did help us to cover women from different occupational, cultural and socio-religious groups.

2.4.2 Sample Profile

The sample profile is given in Table 2.2. Although the recruitment criterion for the survey was 21–45 years, the majority of respondents are in the 26–40 year age

Table 2.2 Profile of respondents of primary survey

Age of respondent	Percent	Age at first marriage	Percent
23–25 years	2.6	15–20 years	10.5
26–30 years	20.2	21–25 years	50.2
31–35 years	31.6	26–30 years	33.8
36–40 years	31.1	31–35 years	4.8
41 years and Above	14.5	36–40 years	0.7
Religion	*Percent*	*Caste*	*Percent*
Others	8.7	Disadvantaged Castes	9.1
Hindu	91.3	General	90.9
Language	*Percent*	*Living children*	*Percent*
Others	6.6	No children	16.9
Bengali	93.4	At least one children	83.1
Education of respondent	*Percent*	*Education of husband*	*Percent*
Graduate	51.2	Graduate	62.4
PG and Above	20.2	PG and Above	12.3
Professional	9.0	Professional	17.8
PG Diploma	19.6	Diploma courses/Others	7.5
Occupation of respondent	*Percent*	*Residential area*	*Percent*
Housewife	20.0	South Kolkata	32.2
Teachers	24.1	North Kolkata	26.2
Clerks	12.3	Salt Lake	3.5
Managers	5.0	Suburban areas	38.1
Professionals	10.1		
Business	28.5		

group. Over 80 % of them had been married within 21–30 years. About one-tenth of the respondents were married by the age of 20 years. Hindus (91 %) and General Castes (91 %) comprise most of the respondents. About 93 % of respondents belong to the Bengali-speaking respondents. About 50 % of the respondents are graduates and 20 % postgraduates; only 9 % have professional qualifications. While over 60 % of respondents have husbands who are graduates, corresponding figures for respondents with husbands having postgraduate degree and professional qualifications are 12 and 12 %, respectively. About 83 % of respondents have at least one child. About 43 % have one living son, while 4 % have two living sons. Corresponding figures for living daughters are 39 and 4 %, respectively. One out of every five respondents is housewife. Quite a few of the respondents are either involved in business (29 %) or are teachers in schools/colleges/universities (24 %). About 12 % of respondents are involved in clerical jobs, while one out of every ten respondents is a professional.

2.5 Methodology

2.5.1 Steps in Analysis

The analysis starts with a bivariate analysis of NFHS data. Traditional contraceptive prevalence rates among women of different socio-economic stratum (classified by parity, age, religion, caste, education, employment status, profile of partner, etc.) are estimated to identify the socio-economic groups commonly using traditional methods. Parametric and non-parametric tests are undertaken to test the hypotheses that users of traditional contraceptives are more efficient in keeping fertility low. We then explore the bivariate relationship between contraceptive use and gender parity, along the lines suggested by Jayaraman et al. (2009). This is followed by estimation of a multinomial logit model regressing contraceptive choice on parity and gender composition of living children, taking socio-economic and demographic profile as the control variables. Details of the functional form and sample are given in Chap. 3.

Chapters 4 and 5 discuss the results of analysis of the quantitative data from the primary survey. Chapter 4 follows the standard format of earlier chapters—examining the extent of reliance on behavioural methods across different correlates. This analysis is followed by an attempt to correlate contraceptive choice with parity. We next undertake an econometric analysis to identify factors influencing choice of behavioural methods. As the dependent variable is binary (the choice is between use of modern methods and use of behavioural methods), a logit model is the appropriate econometric model. This model is estimated for the sample of respondents using any contraceptive method—dropping respondents not using any methods. In addition, two other models are estimated—(a) a logit model explaining reliance on each of the two variants of behavioural methods, withdrawal and rhythm; and (b) a sequential logit[1] modelling the decision-making process in two steps—first, whether to use modern method or behavioural method, followed by the choice between withdrawal and rhythm.

Such traditional methods of analysis, however, are not suitable to analyse some of the issues raised by us. In particular, if we have to address the deficiencies produced by the focus on current and ever use, the narrow set of factors supposedly determining contraception choice and the static framework used, we have to shift to a more dynamic approach that examines combinations of contraception method, and how they change with conceptions. The initial analysis (undertaken in Chap. 5) is centred around studying the combination that is most popular, how use of combination changes with age and the reasons underlying choice of combinations. Since the focus is on transitions, we have also used a new tool that has not been previously used in demographic research to study contraception choice. This is a transition matrix that depicts the transition between one combination to another over different conceptions. The final part of the analysis is an econometric exercise to identify possible determinants of contraception combinations. Since the combination of methods forms a categorical variable, the econometric analysis is based on a multinomial logit model

2.5.2 *Qualitative Analysis*

In addition to statistical analysis of questionnaire-based data, we also planned to undertake detailed interviews of selected women. The value of such ethnographic information, although not amenable to statistical analysis, is immense in drawing out supplementary information. The problem with employing such methods in urban areas is the natural wariness of urban residents and reluctance to confide in strangers. This becomes a major problem when the information is confidential and personal. In addition to social taboos, individual-level factors also become important. Shyness and the reluctance to confide personal matters to a stranger create a barrier in undertaking interviews relating to reproductive behaviour. Only prolonged interaction on a daily basis, with the investigator residing as part of the community, can break the distrust and suspicion. While this is possible in case of rural communities, or in urban slums, the residential and living patterns of urban graduates makes efforts to break down barriers of confidentiality between the investigators and respondents difficult. Hence, we designed some additional questions seeking information on reproductive and sexual behaviour. Such questions

[1]Sequential logit model is a typical variant of a multinomial logit model when the polychotomous response variable Y is not only ordered, but also has a hierarchical structure. This implies that the model proceeds as if decisions were made in a sequence of stages.

were put forward to women who were more vocal or forward. The responses to the questions are reported in Chap. 6 and provide evidence in support of the risk society hypothesis.

References

Basu, A. M. (2005). Ultramodern contraception: Social class and family planning in India. *Asian Population Studies, 1*(3), 303–323.

Jayaraman, A., Mishra, V., & Arnold, F. (2009). The relationship of family size and composition to fertility desires, contraceptive adoption and method choice in South Asia. *International Perspectives on Sexual and Reproductive Health, 35*(1), 29–38.

Roy, T. K., Jayachandran, V., & Banerjee, S. (1999). Economic condition and fertility: Is there a relationship? *Economic and Political Weekly, 3*(42–43), 3041–3046.

Chapter 3
Ultra-modernism or Son Preference?

Analysis of NFHS Data

Abstract This chapter examines the first explanation of high reliance on behavioural contraceptive methods—the theory of "ultra-modern contraception"—based on an analysis of National Family Health Survey (NFHS) unit-level data. Analysis of all-India data reveals that a low but increasing proportion of women rely on behavioural methods. Such women are predominantly from the urban, educated, and affluent class. Further, reliance on behavioural methods is exceptionally high among Bengali-speaking respondents and respondents from East Indian states. Analysis of data from West Bengal, in particular, reveals that one out of every five women were current users of behavioural method in 1992–1993; this proportion has increased to 30 % by 2005–2006. Prima facie, users of behavioural methods are able to regulate fertility satisfactorily. Statistical tests, however, castes aspersions on the supposed efficiency of such methods. Users of behavioural methods have reported higher number of induced abortions. The relationship between contraceptive choice and gender parity indicates that reliance on traditional contraceptives may be a temporary phase occurring before attainment of desired family size and gender composition. The analysis of NFHS data, thus, refutes the "ultra-modern" contraception hypothesis.

Keywords Behavioural methods · Induced abortions · Multinomial logit · Ultra-modern contraception · Urban elite

Z. Husain and M. Dutta, *Fertility Control in a Risk Society*,
SpringerBriefs in Population Studies, DOI 10.1007/978-81-322-3685-6_3

3.1 Theory of Ultra-modern Contraception[1]

The crux of the ultra-modern contraception theory is that emerging forms of femininity and their contradictions with Western ideologies lead women to adopt non-invasive, non-biomedical traditional methods such as coitus interruptus, rhythm, and conventional contraceptive methods (condoms).[2]

3.1.1 Behavioural Methods as a Form of Cultural Dissent

Basu (2005) starts by using NFHS data to challenge the notion that behavioural methods are used by only a negligible proportion of Indian women, that too from the low income, uneducated, and rural residents. While the overall contraceptive prevalence rate in India is 40.6, 5.8 % of currently married urban women aged 15–49 practise withdrawal and the rhythm methods. Upon adding condom users, this figure increases to 11.6 %. In contrast, only 1.2 % of currently married rural women aged 15–49 practise withdrawal and rhythm; the figure rises to only 5 % on adding condom users. The ranges become more striking when one disaggregates women by education and age. Traditional methods account for 62 % of total contraceptive use among urban women aged 20–29 and with a college degree, compared to 13 % among rural illiterate women. For women aged 30–34, the figures are 52 and 7 %.

As behavioural methods are practiced by "elites"—who have both the skill and knowledge to use such methods reliably—Basu warns that the use of such methods should not be equated with traditional attitudes or ignorance. In fact, she argues that, citing data from NFHS-1, "users of traditional methods end up with *lower* fertility than the average for their group as a whole *as well as* users of the more effective methods such as sterilization." (Basu 2005: 308, emphasis in the original).

Moreover, Basu continues, the use of behavioural methods is motivated by modern attitudes, especially about femininity, the female body, and reproductive processes, and, therefore, the practice of such forms of birth control is a mark of a modern society.

Basu (2005) explains the increasing adoption of behavioural methods among the urban elite in terms of a reaction against the "misplaced modernity" spreading among poorer women. Such women view the body as a functional unit to be used

[1]This chapter is based on Husain et al. (2013). Reproduced with permission.

[2]Condoms are considered a "traditional" form of contraception because "condoms have existed and been in use for centuries, but also because they are non-invasive and because they are among the most 'inefficient' methods of pregnancy prevention in all the standard evaluation models of family planning programmes" (Basu 2005: 304–305). During our subsequent data analysis, however, we use "traditional" or "behavioural" contraceptive methods to refer only to withdrawal and rhythm.

for basic sociocultural and economic tasks subject to interference from menstruation and pregnancies. So, once the desired family size is attained, the two processes tend to be seen as burdensome and things that women wish could be done away with (Uberoi and Bahadur 2001). This attitude encourages interest in modern contraceptive methods that can be easily used—particularly if one of the side effects is to reduce the intensity of the menstrual cycle. The intrusion of the state into the daily private life of women becomes a welcome process as the medicalization of the body occurs through the public provisioning of reproductive health-related services that provide relief from pregnancy and menstruation.

The demand for ultra-modern contraception emerges as a reaction to such misplaced modernism, through the emergence of postmodern attitudes among urban, educated women. Instead of viewing the body as a functional producer unit, it is increasingly being viewed as a temple that must be nurtured and protected. The body is conceptualized as a consumer unit; thereby, the focus shifts from ritual purity of the body to personal hygiene (Puri 1999). This growing "body consciousness" (Uberoi and Bahadur 2001) among the urban elite leads to negative opinions about scientific- and technology-based modern means and positive attitudes toward natural, eco-friendly products. In the case of reproductive behaviour, this encourages urban, educated, "ultra-modern" women to shun modern contraceptive methods associated with Western science and technology and adopt family control methods that are natural, less invasive, in tune with emerging forms of femininity—and linked with tradition and the past.

3.1.2 Traditional Contraception as Natural Method—New Forms of Modernity

Basu's work is in line with contemporary research on traditional contraception. Such works point out that contraception may be used to attain social goals other than merely preventing pregnancy. This calls for an examination of the cultural context in which the contraceptive choice is made (Johnson-Hanks 2002).

In Sicilian society, for instance, it is associated with disciplined, honourable, and modern identity (Schneider and Schneider 1996). The Beti honour complex—focusing on self-possession, autonomy, and self-discipline—encourages the practice of abstinence in Cameroon (Johnson-Hanks 2005). In Tuscany, Krause observes a desire to domesticate desire underlying the use of withdrawal—"in contrast to peasant sexuality, a key symbol of modern sexual relation was control" (Krause 2005: 121). In contrast, by relaxing the need for discretion and social decorum, modern methods encourage sexual vagabonds (Johnson-Hanks 2002).

In the Sicilian study, the wives viewed the practice of withdrawal in a positive light, expressing gratitude to husbands who "had this much respect," and praising husbands for being *cosciente* (conscious, aware), for withdrawing "beautifully, precisely, exactly," for having *tanto volunta* (so much will) (Schneider and

Schneider 1991: 894). Elmendorf (1979: 419) argues similarly that many women feel they are "being taken care of" when their husbands practice withdrawal.

Evidence also exists that the necessity for male restraint required by withdrawal is sometimes experienced positively by men. The Sicilian study found that men perceive coitus interruptus as "a learned skill … and a source of pride to those who did it successfully." Users boasted that "the train can go forward, the train can go backward." Users among all classes associated withdrawal with some sacrifice, but also with a "respectable way of life" (Schneider and Schneider 1991: 889). Ramaswamy and Smith (1976: 76) note that "For some couples, this method is very successful. In these cases, the man has great control over his functions, a protective attitude, and is happy to be in command of the situation."

Users in such societies often perceive the distinction to be between natural and artificial (technological) forms of birth control (Johnson-Hanks 2005: 242) rather than between modern and traditional. Rutenberg and Watkins (1997) report the concern expressed by women that invasive technological forms of birth control may lead to side effects and disrupt the natural rhythm of the body. This may lead to fears that such methods may prevent future wanted pregnancies—rather than current unwanted pregnancies (Bledsoe 1996). Such behaviour may be encouraged by gynaecologists emphasizing the negative side effects of methods such as pills and IUDs or by misinformation spread within social networks dominated by ideologies linking femininity with maternity (Dalla Zuanna et al. 2005). Users of withdrawal and abstinence often take recourse to a "discourse of naturalism" while explaining their choice (Gribaldo et al. 2009). Narratives by traditional contraception users equate such methods with nature, health, and well-being (Johnson-Hanks 2002).

Finally, in societies characterized by unequal gender relations, the medicalization of women's bodies by invasive biomedical methods has been criticized as "the ultimate manifestation of patriarchal power" (Dalla Zuanna et al. 2005: 45). In contrast, behavioural methods conform to ideals of natural maternity and are spontaneous, flexible, negotiable, and based upon communication between partners (Gribaldo et al. 2009).

> In contrast to the multiple dangers inherent in 'contraception', coitus interruptus was sometimes described as a 'more natural' *[pio fisiologhiko; piofisiko]* method of birth control. Pills and the IUD, in contrast, were sometimes called 'unnatural'. It has been suggested … that what makes coitus interruptus 'natural' and, thus preferable, for Greek women is the possibility of conception it leaves open: since sex and conception are regarded as inseparable, without the possibility of pregnancy, women could not experience sex as pleasurable or desirable (Georges 1996: 514).

The contention that reliance on behavioural methods signifies the persistence of patriarchal norms and male dominance in sexual relations has also been questioned. Discussions with Rhodian women suggest that while it is true that reliance on coitus interruptus is a means of "pass(ing) the responsibility of birth control to men" (Loizos and Papataxiarchis 1991), it is equally true that women's assertions of their own needs are often necessary to ensure men's effective cooperation (Flandrin 1979; Mclaren 1990; Petchesky 1990).

Interviews with Greek women suggest a sense that use of behavioural methods represents a sacrifice of the husband's pleasure (Georges 1996):

> Smaro, 24 years old, was blunt: "so let the man's pleasure be diminished" A hospital social worker who frequently counselled Rhodians on contraception summarized women's feelings toward the use of coitus interruptus as a major means of birth control by using the common Greek expression: "why me, and not him?" *(ghiati egho ke ohi ekinos?)*. In other words, she explained, why should I be the one to take the health risks and bear the discomforts of contraception?" (Georges 1996: 514).

Gribaldo et al. (2009) reports that, in Italy, women do not view withdrawal in terms of dependence on the male partner, his self-control, and his sexual priorities. Rather, as withdrawal is the product of a deep partnership between men and women, its use reflects a profound trust in the male partner who has the responsibility of sacrificing his sexual pleasure by control of his sexual instincts. Giacobazzi et al. study (1989) brings out that withdrawal is not just a contraception method to Italian couples, but an expression of intimacy.[3]

3.2 A Critical Assessment

Basu's work challenges conventional notions about the motivations guiding adoption of behavioural contraceptive methods and their supposed ineffectiveness in controlling fertility. Her emphasis on the postmodern attitude of users and a substitution of the modern/traditional dichotomy by the natural/technological discourse provides an alternative perspective in the literature on reproductive health. This work focuses on an issue that is not an isolated regional phenomenon but may also be situated in a global context. Data on contraception choice in other countries (see Table 1.1) show that behavioural methods are commonly used in many countries—including non-Islamic and developed countries. Studies of fertility changes in Europe have shown that behavioural methods have played a major role in the demographic transition in the era before invasive methods and pills were discovered. Even now, in countries such as Italy, a high proportion of couples continue to rely on behavioural contraception. Understanding the profile of users of behavioural methods and identifying the motivations guiding their choice is an important exercise in demography.

Despite the intellectual and theoretical strength of her work, Basu fails to fully consider the complexity, characterizing the change in fertility behaviour (Roy et al. 1999)—particularly the persistent influence of traditional forces despite the advent of modern Western attitudes.

First, the factors determining the choice of behavioural methods need to be analysed to understand the reasons for choosing a contraceptive method. In the

---

[3]The study found that 78 % of women viewed communication as the primary goal of sexual relationships.

absence of statistical or ethnographic evidence, Basu's extension of the emerging anthropological and psychological literature on women's attitudes, ranging from those toward the body to family planning in India, is speculative—despite its intellectual worth. It is also inconsistent with studies of how women's experience of their bodies is shaped by the media and the fashion/beauty industry (Thapan 1997).

Second, contraceptive choice is conceptualized in static terms—the possibility that preferences may shift over different phases of the reproductive life cycle is ignored. In particular, Basu (2005) does not consider the possibility that women may adopt modern methods during their peak reproductive years and switch to periodic abstinence afterwards (Nashid et al. 2007). Similarly, women with unsatisfied fertility desires may rely on behavioural methods; subsequently, after attaining the desired parity and gender composition, they may shift to modern forms of birth control. There is considerable ethnographic evidence that couples may use behavioural methods as a transitory method when they are ambivalent about pregnancy (Gribaldo et al. 2009) or undecided about its timing (Fisher 2000) or simply want to ensure spontaneity of conception (Gribaldo et al. 2009).

This implies that it would be misleading

> … to consider the choice of a method at a point in time as representing the only choice that couples will make during their reproductive careers. More specifically, a couple might choose 'traditional' methods at some stages of the family life cycle and 'modern' methods at other stages (Gray et al. 1997: 15).

Data from the NFHS-3 reveal that behavioural contraceptive users comprise a large section of currently married urban elite women (urban women with above secondary levels of education and belonging to the highest standard of living quintile class) of West Bengal, India. About 29 % of women wanting a child within two years and about 43 % of women wanting a child but unsure about the timing and about 32 % of women who were undecided were using behavioural contraceptive methods. The corresponding figures for users of the modern method are 18.3, 14.3, and 40.9 %. In contrast, about half the women wanting a child after two years currently use modern contraceptive methods (50.8 %), while 35.2 % use behavioural methods.

It should also be noted that a strong son preference guides contraceptive choice and fertility preferences in India (Arnold 2001; Jayaraman et al. 2009; Dutta and Husain 2011). It is quite possible that users who have unsatisfied fertility desires, particularly for sons, and are ambivalent about the timing of conception use behavioural practices as a transitory method. This is important, as son preference and sex selection is dominant among the urban elite (Jha et al. 2011; Nanda and Véron 2005). This may explain the lower number of CEB for women using behavioural methods compared to women using modern methods, as observed by Basu (2005). Fertility levels of women not using a contraceptive are even lower among women aged 30–34 (Table 4, in Basu [2005])—a point her analysis overlooks.

Further, Basu's conclusions about the effectiveness of "ultra-modern" methods are based on an analysis of the number of living children rather than on an actual number of pregnancies. Her study does not consider the possibility that lack of knowledge and skill may also lead women to take recourse to emergency contraception and induced abortions—that are biomedical processes—to adhere to fertility plans (Fisher 2000; Johnson-Hanks 2002; Erfani and Yuksel-Kaptanoglu 2012; Nguyen and Miller 2012). The use of any variant of the rhythm method requires a degree of knowledge of the physiological process of conception and the stages of the ovulatory/menstrual cycle and considerable interspousal communication. Data from the NFHS-3 reveal that 60.4 % of the urban elite who use behavioural contraception and 72.6 % of those who use modern methods do not know the ovulatory cycle. Lack of knowledge and skill may lead to unintended pregnancies (Gray et al. 1997). In such cases, the couple may have to rely on emergency contraception or go for induced abortion, which are certainly not "natural" (a point that the literature on behavioural methods often ignores; see, for example, Basu 2005; Johnson-Hanks 2002) and adversely affect the woman's reproductive health, fecundity, and mental health.[4] Based on data from the Philippines, Juarez et al. (2009: 3–4) notes that women using modern methods "account for a disproportionately large share of women seeking an abortion." In a study of contraception in Italy—where withdrawal had been used successfully to control fertility at the start of the twentieth century—Castiglioni et al. (2001) advocates caution

> before assuming that Italians are the masters and mistresses of their own fertility, particularly if conceptions rather than births are considered. In Italy during the 1990s, 37 % of conceptions were unplanned (at least at occurrence), reaching 45 % among under 20 and over 35 years old women. For older women abortion rates are higher compared with other Western countries (230).

Similarly, data from the NFHS-3 reveal that within the group of currently married urban women with at least higher secondary education and belonging to the top two standard of living quintile groups in West Bengal, 18.2 % of women using behavioural family planning methods users have had pregnancies medically terminated compared to 15.9 % among users of modern methods and 17.9 % in the group as a whole. In India as a whole, the corresponding figures are 25.1, 20.7, and 20.5 %, respectively. In fact, the incidence of medically terminated pregnancies among users of behavioural methods is even higher than among non-users (18.8 %) and marginally lower than among users of folkloric methods (26.5 %). Mukherjee (2009) also observed a high incidence of induced abortions among users of behavioural contraceptive methods during a primary study of West Bengal women. A recent study by Dude et al. (2013) found that users of withdrawal were more likely to have an unintended pregnancy. This not only raises questions about the efficiency of ultra-modern contraception but implies that the use of such methods may have adverse health consequences—as seen in Japan (Sato and Iwasawa 2006) and Nigeria (Otoide et al. 2001).

[4]In addition, if the woman has more than one sexual partner, using traditional methods may increase the probability of RTI/STI and HIV/AIDS.

The above discussion brings into question Basu's explanation of the high prevalence of behavioural birth control methods and her conceptualization of the issue of ultra-modern contraception in India. This study re-examines the issue of the high prevalence of behavioural family planning methods. While accepting Basu's proposition that ultra-modern methods are mainly used by urban, educated, and well-off families, the paper argues that the use of behavioural birth control methods may not reflect elitism or modern attitudes. The use of such behavioural methods is more reflective of ambivalence about the timing of conception among those who have not yet attained the desired family size or the gender composition of children, and consequently, the use of behavioural methods is transitory. The report starts with an all-India-level analysis but subsequently concentrates on West Bengal, a major state in India. The reason is the high prevalence of behavioural methods in this state (34.2 % among women at risk).

3.3 Re-Examining All-India Data

Our estimates reveal that 6.8 % of currently married women aged 15–49 use behavioural methods of family planning. Round-wise estimates indicate that usage of such methods has increased over the three rounds—4.0 % (1992–93), 6.3 % (1998–99), and 8.6 % (2005–06). Bivariate analysis (Table 3.1) reveals that the usage of such methods is relatively higher among urban women, educated women (with secondary or higher levels of education), those employed in the tertiary sector, women aged 20–39, women with partners educated beyond secondary levels or engaged in tertiary sector jobs, women from affluent households (belonging to the top two quintiles of standard of living), and Muslims.

Figures for the urban educated and affluent class—Basu's elite—also reveal that one out of every ten currently married women relies on behavioural family planning methods (10.4 %). Analysis of the *trend over period of study*, however, shows an

Table 3.1 Percentage of currently married women using behavioural methods among socio-economic groups in India

Socio-economic correlates		1992–1993	1998–1999	2005–2006
Place of residence	Urban	4.8	8.7	9.4
	Rural	3.5	5.2	8.1
Highest education of respondent	No education	2.1	3.9	6.2
	Primary	3.8	5.5	7.3
	Secondary	6.1	8.7	10.5
	Higher	7.6	13.9	14.0
Occupation of respondent	Unemployed	4.6	7.2	9.3
	Primary	2.0	3.4	6.5
	Tertiary	4.1	11.1	10.8

(continued)

Table 3.1 (continued)

Socio-economic correlates		1992–1993	1998–1999	2005–2006
Grouped age of respondents	13–19 years	15.7	3.8	7.2
	20–29 years	5.1	6.2	9.0
	30–39 years	3.6	7.4	9.7
	40–50 years	2.6	5.6	6.8
Highest education of partner	No education	2.1	3.6	5.9
	Primary	2.8	4.8	6.7
	Secondary	4.7	6.6	9.2
	Higher	6.0	10.7	13.0
Occupation of partner	Unemployed	3.4	6.2	7.6
	Primary	3.0	5.1	7.6
	Tertiary	4.6	9.0	10.4
Grouped age of partners	10–25 years	8.2	4.1	7.5
	26–30 years	5.4	5.8	8.7
	31–40 years	3.9	7.2	9.3
	41–50 years	3.5	6.9	9.0
	50 and above	2.5	4.7	6.0
Grouped Standard of Living Index (SLI)	Poorest	2.5	4.0	5.7
	Poor	3.0	4.7	7.5
	Rich	4.3	7.7	9.4
	Richest	5.6	9.9	10.4
Socio-religious identity	H-SC	2.8	5.0	8.2
	H-ST	2.2	3.5	4.8
	Muslim	5.6	6.7	9.4
	Others	4.6	7.9	8.9

increase between the first two rounds, after which it becomes constant—6.7 % (1992–93), 11.9 % (1998–99), and 11.2 % (2005–06). Moreover, it should be noted that these figures are high only in a *relative* sense. In no case, is the percentage greater than 16 %. Out of the 96 cells of Table 3, in only 9 cases is the value greater than 10 %, while in 35 cases it is less than 5 %.

3.4 Contraception Use in West Bengal

Basu (2005) considers these figures high enough to arrive at strong conclusions about changes in reproductive behaviour linked to cultural dissent and reaction against Western influences within a society that is otherwise more than keen to adopt Western practices. If one looks at state-wise figures, however, the above figures are quite low compared to figures for West Bengal, Assam, Tripura, and

Table 3.2 State-wise variations in behavioural contraceptive prevalence rate among currently married women

State	1992–93	1998–99	2005–06
Andhra Pradesh	0.6	0.5	0.7
Assam	49.2	17.0	28.8
Bihar	5.8	1.6	5.8
Jharkhand	NA	NA	4.9
Gujarat	4.9	5.6	10.0
Haryana	11.3	8.8	4.8
Himachal Pradesh	7.7	7.5	1.8
Jammu and Kashmir	20.0	6.9	7.9
Karnataka	3.4	1.7	1.0
Kerala	14.0	7.7	10.7
Madhya Pradesh	2.1	1.3	3.0
Chhattisgarh	NA	NA	3.0
Maharashtra	2.1	1.6	2.0
Manipur	30.9	12.6	25.6
Orissa	3.4	5.8	5.6
Punjab	12.4	12.8	7.1
Rajasthan	2.5	2.0	2.4
Tamil Nadu	8.1	2.3	1.5
Tripura	48.3	11.4	20.9
Uttar Pradesh	6.0	5.4	12.7
Uttaranchal	NA	NA	3.9
West Bengal	35.2	21.5	23.3
All India	**11.6**	**5.8**	**8.1**

Note Chhattisgarh, Jharkhand, and Uttarakhand were merged with Madhya Pradesh, Bihar, and Uttar Pradesh, respectively

Manipur (see Table 3.2).[5] In particular, figures for West Bengal, a state with 44.4 million women, comprising 7.6 % of the female population of the country are worth noting.

The extremely high reliance on behavioural contraceptive methods in West Bengal among all socio-economic groups is worth studying. In particular, it is high among urban residents, respondents with more than 10 years of schooling, respondents engaged in tertiary sector, women aged below 40, with partners aged 26–50, working in the tertiary sector or with more than 10 years of schooling, respondents belonging to top two quintile groups and belonging to Hindu-Other[6] and Other[7] communities. Table 3.3 also reveals that urban women with more than 10 years of schooling and belonging to the top two quintile groups demonstrate

[5]The sharp drop in 1998–1999 is a peculiarity for reproductive information in NFHS-2.

[6]Hindu-Other consists of Hindu respondents belonging to upper caste and other backward caste groups, and does not include Scheduled Castes and Tribes.

[7]'Others' comprises non-Muslim religious minorities, such as Christians, Sikhs, and Parsis.

Table 3.3 Percentage of currently married women using behavioural methods among socio-economic groups in West Bengal, India

Socio-economic groups		West Bengal			Urban elite in West Bengal[a]		
		1992–93	1998–99	2005–06	1992–93	1998–99	2005–06
Type of place of residence	Urban	20.2	30.0	28.8			
	Rural	13.1	17.0	20.1			
Highest education of respondent	No education	8.0	12.3	16.4			
	Primary	16.1	19.7	19.7			
	Secondary	22.0	30.8	31.1			
	Higher	30.5	44.4	40.2			
Occupation of respondent	Unemployed	16.6	24.5	26.4	34.0	45.9	37.5
	Primary	4.8	14.0	17.2	–	100.0	50.0
	Tertiary	9.7	25.2	24.7	26.3	43.6	42.2
Highest education of partner	No education	9.0	11.8	16.6	–	25.0	–
	Primary	9.6	18.0	18.4	–	–	–
	Secondary	16.5	24.2	28.5	37.5	37.8	47.5
	Higher	28.1	39.1	35.0	32.7	46.8	38.0
Grouped age of respondents	13–19 years	37.8	28.9	25.6	–	20.0	–
	20–29 years	18.3	23.3	24.8	35.0	34.7	26.0
	30–39 years	10.6	23.3	26.9	34.0	51.6	47.0
	40–50 years	8.5	19.5	20.1	28.6	48.3	37.6
Occupation of partner	Unemployed	10.9	24.1	18.4	–	34.3	100.0
	Primary	13.2	19.1	21.0	–	51.4	50.0
	Tertiary	16.1	28.8	30.0	33.1	46.4	37.8
Grouped age of partners	10–25 years	30.7	23.9	24.0	–	–	–
	26–30 years	20.7	25.6	24.4	27.3	35.7	30.0
	31–40 years	14.9	23.2	25.6	38.6	44.3	38.8
	41–50 years	11.0	23.2	25.7	32.0	50.0	49.0
	50 and above	7.4	16.9	19.3	23.1	49.2	23.3
Grouped SLI	Poorest	10.0	13.9	13.6			
	Poor	10.4	17.4	23.1			
	Middle	11.1	20.9	24.7			
	Rich	20.7	29.7	33.7			
	Richest	23.7	35.9	32.8			
Socio-religious identity	H-SC	8.2	15.7	20.8	–	36.4	42.1
	H-ST	6.3	9.7	17.3	33.1	46.3	40.2
	H-Others	15.9	27.9	28.0	–	37.5	25.0
	Muslim	14.7	19.3	21.3	–	40.0	23.1
	Others	20.0	15.5	28.8	–	36.4	42.1

Note [a]Elite refers to women with at least secondary level of education, belonging to top two SLI quintiles and residing in urban areas

greater reliance on behavioural birth control methods. It is not that the pattern of variation differs between West Bengal and India as a whole—what we observe is a marked accentuation of patterns observed for the India sample in West Bengal. Figures are "blown up"—doubling, trebling, and increasing by five or ten times, compared to figures for all India.[8]

A comparison of Tables 3.1 and 3.3 clearly reveals the stark contrast in levels of behavioural contraception use between West Bengal and India. In particular, in line with Basu's findings, we find that educated women belonging to affluent households and residing in urban areas rely to a substantial extent on behavioural methods of family planning. Basu had further argued that, given the socio-economic characteristics of such users, behavioural methods will be quite effective. Let us now turn to an examination of this proposition.

3.5 Efficiency of Ultra-Modern Contraception

The "efficiency" of ultra-modern contraception is tested on the basis of four fertility-related variables:

(a) Number of children ever born,
(b) Number of living sons,
(c) Number of living daughters, and
(d) Number of living children.

Differences in these variables—and whether these differences are statistically significant—across users of modern and behavioural contraception methods are examined as shown in Table 3.4. Basu (2005) had examined differences in fertility between users of behavioural and modern methods using mean. If we compare mean values and testing for differences using the t-ratio, behavioural contraception users appear to be more efficient in keeping fertility low. However, a problem with mean is that it may be influenced by extreme values. This problem may be avoided by comparing median, and using Kruskal–Wallis H-test (which also avoids the assumption of normal distribution). Table 3.4 shows that the number of children ever born, number of living children, and number of livings sons is greater among the users of modern methods, but difference in number of living daughters is not statistically significant even at 5 % level. Further, on examining statistical differences in these variables in each round,[9] or between respondents grouped by marital duration,[10] we found a similar pattern.

---

[8]Figures increase by more than 5 times in 45 cases, and by more than 10 times in 10 instances.

[9]For NFHS-1, differences in only children ever born were found to be significant—differences in other variables were insignificant even at 10 % level.

[10]Respondents were classified by marital duration into three groups—0–5 years, 6–10 years, and rest. The t-ratio indicated significantly higher fertility levels (except for number of living daughters) among women using modern methods for all groups. With respect to the number of

Table 3.4 Differences in fertility-related variables between users of modern and behavioural contraception among urban elite of West Bengal—Merged data

Fertility indicator	Mean			Median		
	Behavioural method	Modern method	t-ratio	Behavioural method	Modern method	Kruskal-Wallis H-ratio
Total children ever born	2.69	3.40	41.85**	2	3	76.62**
No of living children	2.48	3.09	39.94**	2	3	58.58**
No of living sons	1.25	1.68	44.17**	1	2	52.83**
No of living daughters	1.23	1.41	16.11**	1	1	2.87

Note **denotes significance at 1 % level

The differences in parity—or their absence—do not necessarily reflect differences in efficiency of contraceptive methods. In particular, we should consider the possibility that use of traditional contraception is a temporary phase in the reproductive cycle of women, occurring when they have not attained their ideal family size and composition. This implies that women who have not attained desired family size and composition and are not overly concerned with getting pregnant will use traditional contraceptives to avoid side effects of modern methods; once they attain the optimal family size and composition, they will shift to modern methods, which are more reliable. This hypothesis may be checked by comparing differences in age, gap between actual and ideal children, and gender parity between users of traditional and contraceptive methods.

Mean ages of users of behavioural and modern contraception methods are 34 and 33 years, respectively. Although the age difference is statistically significant ($t = 2.5$, $p = 0.1$), the age gap does not indicate that the users are in two distinct phases of reproductive cycle.[11] We also find that 21 % of women using behavioural methods want an additional child; this is higher than the proportion of women using modern methods and wanting an additional child (17 %).[12] Probing further, we find that the gap in actual number of sons (daughters) and ideal number of sons

(Footnote 10 continued)

living daughters, difference in fertility levels was significant only for the last group (married for more than 11 years). Similar findings were observed for the Kruskal–Wallis H-tests, with one difference. For women married less than 6 years, no statistically significant differences in fertility levels were found for any of the indicators.

[11]If individual Rounds are considered, age of users are as follows: Round 1: Traditional method: 32, Modern method: 32, $t = 0.65$; Round 2: Traditional method: 34, Modern method: 33, $t = 1.23$; Round 3: Traditional method: 35, Modern method: 33, $t = 2.94$.

[12]These percentages are 29.9 and 15.4 (Round 1), 18.9 and 15.1 (Round 2), and 21 and 20.7 (Round 3).

Table 3.5 Gender parity and contraceptive choice among urban elite of West Bengal, over each NFHS Round

Parity	1992–1993		1998–1999		2005–2006	
	Behavioural	Modern	Behavioural	Modern	Behavioural	Modern
No child	32.6	46.9	25.0	15.2	26.0	29.9
(1, 0)	–	–	56.3	24.7	48.6	34.1
(1, 1)	–	–	46.9	35.4	43.4	42.1
(2, 0)	–	100.0	44.1	33.8	43.8	37.5
(2, 1)	22.2	22.2	35.2	45.1	30.0	49.2
(2, 2)	–	**100.0**	**29.7**	**56.8**	**35.8**	**49.1**
(3, 0)	–	–	45.5	45.5	–	83.3
(3, 1)	20.0	40.0	31.4	48.6	25.0	65.0
(3, 2)	–	**66.7**	**15.6**	**78.1**	**15.4**	**76.9**
(3, 3)	–	–	**42.9**	**57.1**	–	**100.0**
(4+, 0)	–	100.0	–	–	100.0	
(4+, 1)	–	75.0	33.3	53.3	–	50.0
(4+, 2)	–	**100.0**	**17.6**	**76.5**	**25.0**	**50.0**
(4+, 3)	**25.0**	**25.0**	–	**71.4**	–	**66.7**
(4+, 4)	–	–	–	**100.0**	**33.3**	**66.7**

Bold show the parity levels once son preference is satisfied.

(daughters) is positive and statistically significant for both user groups.[13] Thus, both groups of women are exceeding their targeted family size, which does not speak well of the efficiency with which either of the contraception methods are used. However, while the gap between actual and ideal sons is greater for users of modern methods (1.6; t = 3.53), in case of daughters, the difference is negligible (0.05; t = 0.90). This implies, despite faulty targeting by both groups, users of behavioural methods are *relatively better in targeting sons, but not daughters*. This is an odd result and requires close examination of the fertility preference of users.

The concept of gender parity (Jayaraman et al. 2009) is important in this context. This looks at parity—but also considering the gender composition of living children. Based on number of living sons and daughters, we club families by gender parity as follows:

Gender parity = (x, y), when x: No. of living children; y: No. of living sons.

Given the low fertility rates in West Bengal (median number of sons and daughters has been one each in each of the three rounds), the preferred gender parity seems to be (2, 1). The figures in bold in Table 3.5 show the parity levels once son preference is satisfied. Since sample size is small in 1992–1993 (34, compared to 872 and 632 in 1998–1999 and 2005–2006, respectively), we ignore this year. It is interesting to see that women who have attained this targeted gender

[13]Among users of traditional method, gap in actual number of sons (daughters) and ideal number of sons (daughters) is 0.26 (0.09), with t-value of 7.748 (2.714). For users of modern methods, the corresponding numbers are: 0.22 (0.25) and 5.641 (7.622).

parity tend to rely on modern methods less than on behavioural methods. This indicates that reliance on behavioural contraceptive method may be a temporary phase in the reproductive phase of women.

Finally, we should also check the incidence of induced abortions to rule out the fact that inefficiency in use of rhythm and withdrawal is compensated by medical termination of unwanted pregnancies. This is important given that NFHS-3 data show that only 23.1 % of urban elite women using behavioural methods of contraception are aware of when the ovulatory cycle occurs. A higher proportion of users of modern methods has had abortions in 1992–1993 (though the difference is insignificant) and round 2, but this gets reversed in round 3.[14] Nevertheless, as seen earlier, the *number* of induced abortions per women in 2005–2006 is higher among users of behavioural family planning methods. Unfortunately, this variable is not available in earlier rounds.

To sum up, the analysis undertaken in this section raises questions challenging Basu's (2005) claim that ultra-modern contraception methods are more efficient than modern methods. In particular, the relationship between contraceptive choice and gender parity indicates that reliance on traditional contraceptives may be a temporary phase occurring before attainment of desired family size and gender composition, while the relationship between contraceptive choice and induced abortions castes doubts on supposed efficiency of ultra-modern methods.

Now the analysis of gender parity and contraception choice was undertaken without controlling for socio-economic characteristics of respondents. Given the importance of this result for our analysis, we undertake an econometric analysis to test the hypothesis that women shift from behavioural family planning methods to more reliable modern methods once targeted gender parity is attained.

3.6 Multivariate Analysis

3.6.1 Functional Form

Six regression models are estimated. Model 1 is the basic model, identifying determinants of contraceptive choice at the all-India level. Model 2 is estimated by adding a dummy for West Bengal residents, to test whether reliance on behavioural contraceptive methods is indeed greater in West Bengal. Model 3 is Model 1, re-estimated for West Bengal respondents only to confirm that determinants of contraceptive method are not different for this state. In the next step, a dummy for urban elite is added to test whether reproductive choice of this group varies

[14]Proportion of women by contraception method having had abortions are as follows: Round 1: Traditional method: 17 %, Modern method: 20 %, t = −0.60; Round 2: Traditional method: 19 %, Modern method: 29 %, t = −2.85; Round 3: Traditional method: 20 %, Modern method: 14 %, t = 1.94.

significantly from the remaining respondents. Models 4 and 5 are run for West Bengal, using two definitions of "urban elite." In Model 4, "urban elite" refers to urban residents with secondary or higher levels of education—so that definition of "urban elite" corresponds to Basu (2005). In Model 5, the SLI criterion is added—in addition to residing in urban areas and having at least secondary level of education, respondents belong to the top two standard of living groups.

These models are as follows:

$$\text{RV313} = \alpha + \beta_1\ \text{URBAN} + \beta_2\ \text{V012} + \beta_3\ \text{SV012} + \beta_4\ \text{PRIMARY} + \beta_5\ \text{SECONDARY} + \beta_6\ \text{HIGHER} + \beta_7\ \text{P\_PRIMARY} + \beta_8\ \text{P\_SECONDARY} + \beta_9\ \text{HSC} + \beta_{10}\ \text{HST} + \beta_{11}\ \text{MUSLIM} + \beta_{12}\ \text{OTHERS} + \beta_{13}\ \text{LCHILD} + \beta_{14}\ \text{SLIGROUP1} + \beta_{15}\ \text{SLIGROUP2} + \beta_{16}\ \text{SLIGROUP4} + \beta_{17}\ \text{SLIGROUP5} + \beta_{18}\ \text{NFHS2} + \beta_{19}\ \text{NFHS3} + u_i \quad \text{estimated for all India} \quad [1]$$

$$\text{RV313} = \text{MODEL 1} + \beta_{20}\ \text{BENGAL} + u_i \quad \text{estimated for all India} \quad [2]$$

$$\text{RV313} = \text{MODEL 1} \quad \text{estimated for West Bengal sample} \quad [3]$$

$$\text{RV313} = \alpha + \beta 1\ \text{V012} + \beta 3\ \text{SV012} + \beta 7\ \text{P\_PRIMARY} + \beta 8\ \text{P\_SECONDARY} + \beta 9\ \text{HSC} + \beta 10\ \text{HST} + \beta 11\ \text{MUSLIM} + \beta 12\ \text{OTHERS} + \beta 13\ \text{LCHILD} + \beta 14\ \text{NFHS2} + \beta 19\ \text{NFHS3} + + \beta 20\ \text{WBELITE} + u_i \quad \text{estimated for urban elite in West Bengal} \quad [4]$$

$$\text{RV313} = \alpha + \beta 1\ \text{V012} + \beta 3\ \text{SV012} + \beta 7\ \text{P\_PRIMARY} + \beta 8\ \text{P\_SECONDARY} + \beta 9\ \text{HSC} + \beta 10\ \text{HST} + \beta 11\ \text{MUSLIM} + \beta 12\ \text{OTHERS} + \beta 13\ \text{LCHILD} + \beta 14\ \text{NFHS2} + \beta 19\ \text{NFHS3} + + \beta 20\ \text{WBELITE}' + u_i \quad \text{estimated for urban elite in West Bengal} \quad [5]$$

when

RV313: Choice of contraceptive method (1: Not using contraceptive methods and using folkloric method; 2: Using behavioural contraceptive method; 3 Using modern contraceptive method, with base outcome being using behavioural contraceptive method)
URBAN: Respondent residing in urban area
BENGAL: Dummy for respondents residing in West Bengal
V012: Age of respondent
SV012: Square of age of respondent
V512: Marital duration
PRIMARY: Respondent has primary education
SECONDARY: Respondent has primary education
HIGHER: Respondent has primary education
(Reference category: Respondent is illiterate)[15]
HSC: Respondent is Hindu-Scheduled Caste
HST: Respondent is Hindu-Scheduled Tribe

---

[15]Education of only respondent, and not partner, is taken as correlation between these two variables which is very high (0.6098).

MUSLIM: Respondent is Muslim
OTHERS: Respondent is non-Muslim religious minority
(Reference category: Respondent is Hindu Forward Caste)
LCHILD: Number of living child
SLINFHS: Standard of Living Index
NFHS2: Respondent in NFHS-2, 1998–1999
NFHS3: Respondent in NFHS-3, 2005–1906
(Reference category: Respondent in NFHS-1, 1992–1993)
WBELITE: Respondent resides in urban areas and has completed secondary level of education
WBELITE′: Respondent resides in urban areas, has completed secondary level of education, and belongs to top two SLI groups

Although the duration of marriage is a very important determinant of fertility decisions and contraceptive choice, we have not included this among the explanatory variables. The reason is the high correlation between marital duration and age (0.91 at the all-India and West Bengal level) that is likely to cause multicollinearity and distorting results.

3.6.2 Analysis of Econometric Results

The models are estimated for the sample of currently married women who are not currently pregnant. In Models 3 and 4, the sample is reduced further to include only urban elite (urban residents, belonging to fourth and fifth SLI quintiles and with above secondary-level education). Since the dependent variable is categorical (assuming three values), the multinomial logit model is the relevant functional form. The base outcome is taken to be using behavioural contraceptive methods (RV313 = 1). Note that we are reporting relative risk ratios, not coefficients. Results for first five models are reported in Table 3.6. The top panel presents results for not using contraceptives, vis-a-vis using behavioural contraceptives, while the bottom panel reports results for using modern contraceptives, vis-a-vis using behavioural contraceptives. The implication of the results for contraceptive choice is briefly discussed below.

Urban residents prefer modern methods to behavioural methods, while no use is considered the least preferred option. Aged respondents prefer behavioural contraceptives to both not using contraceptives and modern methods, though the relation is not linear. The West Bengal urban elite, however, prefers behavioural methods to not using, while their preference between modern methods and behavioural methods does not change with age. Multivariate analysis indicates behavioural methods become a more preferred means of family planning as education of respondents increases.

Occupation of partner does not have a strong and clear impact on contraceptive choice. From the top panel, we can see that if partners are working in the secondary

Table 3.6 Regression results—All India and West Bengal currently married women

RV313	Model 1: India		Model 2: India		Model 3: Bengal		Model 4: Bengal Elite		Model 5: Bengal Elite	
	RRR	z	RRR	Z	RRR	z	RRR	z	RRR	z
Choice: 0										
WBELITE							0.55	−7.08***		
WBELITE′									0.53	−7.80***
BENGAL			0.14	−48.42***						
URBAN	0.85	−6.28***	0.93	−2.93***	0.78	−2.65**				
V012	0.67	−33.66***	0.67	−33.37***	0.68	−11.30***	0.70	−13.01***	0.70	−12.80***
SV012	1.01	32.82***	1.01	32.84***	1.01	12.04***	1.01	13.65***	1.01	13.47***
PRIMARY	0.63	−12.70***	0.67	−10.90***	0.63	−4.02***				
SECONDARY	0.43	−26.30***	0.44	−25.29***	0.50	−6.01***				
HIGHER	0.33	−24.53***	0.34	−24.02***	0.43	−5.05***	1.11	0.64	1.09	0.52
PRIMARY_P	0.94	−0.90	0.89	−1.69*	0.99	−0.03	1.02	0.10	1.01	0.08
SECONDARY_P	0.89	−1.85*	0.87	−2.15**	1.21	1.02	1.33	3.24***	1.30	2.93***
HSC	0.99	−0.42	1.04	1.10	1.12	1.02	3.16	6.03***	2.98	5.71***
HST	1.55	7.48***	1.47	6.50***	2.54	3.60***	1.77	6.68***	1.73	6.34***
MUSLIM	1.29	7.07***	1.38	8.99***	1.46	3.49***	1.80	2.54**	1.80	2.53**
OTHER	1.29	7.44***	1.15	4.17***	1.78	2.15**	1.04	1.51	1.03	0.99
SLIGROUP1	1.38	8.26***	1.44	9.07***	1.57	3.45***				
SLIGROUP2	1.13	3.36***	1.14	3.53***	1.13	1.00				
SLIGROUP4	0.87	−3.99***	0.84	−4.76***	0.88	−1.09				
SLIGROUP5	0.80	−5.74***	0.72	−8.46***	0.72	−2.22**				
V218	0.92	−9.53***	0.89	−12.95***	0.99	−0.41	0.49	−3.38***	0.49	−3.35***
NFHS2	1.38	3.52***	1.33	3.15***	0.43	−3.44***	0.36	−4.80***	0.38	−4.55***
NFHS3	0.98	−0.25	0.88	−1.39	0.35	−4.13***	0.70	−13.01***	0.70	−12.80***

(continued)

Table 3.6 (continued)

RV313	Model 1: India		Model 2: India		Model 3: Bengal		Model 4: Bengal Elite		Model 5: Bengal Elite	
	RRR	z	RRR	Z	RRR	z	RRR	z	RRR	z
Choice: 2										
WBELITE							0.50	−9.45		
WBELITE′									0.53	−9.15
BENGAL			0.26	-38.47^{***}						
URBAN	1.13	4.81^{***}	1.21	7.54^{***}	0.73	-3.88^{***}				
V012	1.12	9.64^{***}	1.12	9.52^{***}	1.10	2.80^{**}	1.10	3.54	1.10	3.63
SV012	1.00	-7.50^{***}	1.00	-7.12^{***}	1.00	-2.80^{**}	1.00	−3.27	1.00	−3.36
PRIMARY	0.97	−0.94	1.02	0.41	0.81	−2.08				
SECONDARY	0.65	-13.52^{***}	0.66	-12.90^{***}	0.58	-5.33^{***}				
HIGHER	0.42	-19.95^{***}	0.42	-19.64^{***}	0.42	-6.08^{***}	0.95	−0.32	0.94	−0.39
PRIMARY_P	1.13	1.94^{**}	1.08	1.21	0.86	−0.90	0.85	−1.06	0.84	−1.13
SECONDARY_P	0.96	−0.61	0.94	−0.90	0.88	−0.78	1.29	3.37	1.27	3.14
HSC	0.95	−1.56	0.99	−0.33	1.29	2.71^{**}	1.22	1.04	1.16	0.79
HST	1.26	3.98^{***}	1.20	3.13^{***}	1.11	0.40	0.66	−5.23	0.65	−5.42
MUSLIM	0.61	-14.10^{***}	0.64	-12.33^{***}	0.61	-4.92^{***}	0.97	−0.12	0.98	−0.11
OTHER	0.76	-8.12^{***}	0.69	-10.85^{***}	1.16	0.60				
SLIGROUP1	0.95	−1.19	0.98	−0.43	0.95	−0.39				
SLIGROUP2	0.91	-2.58^{**}	0.91	-2.41^{**}	0.87	−1.29				
SLIGROUP4	1.02	0.61	1.00	−0.13	0.78	−2.58				
SLIGROUP5	1.05	1.33	0.96	−1.20	0.89	−0.99	1.34	12.13	1.33	11.63
V218	1.10	10.93^{***}	1.07	7.61^{***}	1.31	9.26^{***}	0.36	−5.35	0.36	−5.36
NFHS2	0.24	-16.97^{***}	0.23	-17.25^{***}	0.32	-5.09^{***}	0.37	−5.17	0.39	−4.94
NFHS3	0.24	-17.02^{***}	0.22	-18.01^{***}	0.40	-4.04^{***}	1.10	3.54	1.10	3.63

(continued)

Table 3.6 (continued)

RV313	Model 1: India		Model 2: India		Model 3: Bengal		Model 4: Bengal Elite		Model 5: Bengal Elite	
	RRR	z	RRR	Z	RRR	z	RRR	z	RRR	z
N	**147,068**		**147,068**		**6719**		**6719**		**6719**	
LR χ^2	**31330.77**		**33486.17**		**1275.73**		**1280.72**		**1277.06**	
PSEUDO R^2	**0.12**		**0.13**		**0.09**		**0.09**		**0.09**	

Note
[1] *Choice 0* "Not using any contraceptives, or using folkloric methods"; *Choice 2* "using modern contraceptive methods"; Base outcome (*Choice 1*) "Using behavioural contraceptive method"
[2] ***denotes $p < 0.01$, **denotes $p < 0.05$, and *denotes $p < 0.10$

sector, behavioural contraceptive methods are preferred, relative to those working in the tertiary sector. West Bengal urban elite women with partners working in the secondary sector prefer not using contraceptives, compared to those with partners working in the tertiary sector. The RRR for those working in the primary sector is significant only in Model 2; the value of the RRR (less than unity) indicates that this group prefers behavioural methods. In the bottom panel, only in Model 1, is coefficient of PRIMARY_P significant. AS the RRR is less than unity, we can infer that this group prefers behavioural methods.

The influence of socio-religious identity on contraceptive choice varies between India and urban elite in West Bengal. While the preferences of HSCs and Hindu Forward Castes (HFCs) do not differ significantly at the all-India level, among the urban elite in West Bengal, a preference against behavioural methods may be observed. HSTs either prefer not to use any methods or prefer to use modern methods for the Indian sample. Muslims and Others prefer not to use any methods, but between behavioural and modern methods, they prefer the former. This may be explained in terms of religious prohibitions and both Islam and certain sects within Christians (such as Roman Catholics and Seventh Day Adventists) disapprove of contraception. Within urban elite of West Bengal, Muslims and Others are found to avoid behavioural contraception, while their choice pattern between behavioural and modern methods does not vary significantly.

Economic status (measured by Standard of Living Index) affects only choice between behavioural methods and not using contraceptives—it does not affect choice between behavioural and modern methods. While respondents belonging to the first two quintiles prefer not using contraceptives, those belonging to the top two quintile groups prefer behavioural methods.

Respondents with larger number of children prefer behavioural methods to not using any method. In case of modern versus behavioural methods, respondents in the Indian sample prefer modern methods, while no significant preference is evinced by the urban elite of West Bengal.

The dummies for NFHS rounds indicate how preference patterns are changing over time. In India, between rounds 1 and 2 (1992–1993 and 1998–1999), there is a shift from behavioural methods to non-use, while there is a shift from modern methods to behavioural methods over the three rounds. In Bengal (Model 3), behavioural methods are becoming more popular over time, though among the urban elite, there is a shift only from no use to behavioural methods.

3.6.3 Gender Parity and Contraception Choice

In Model 2, the Bengal dummy is negative and significant at 1 % level, indicating that respondents from this state prefer behavioural contraception methods. Within West Bengal, urban elite have a strong preference for behavioural contraceptive methods (RRR is less than unity and significant at 1 % level in both Models 4 and 5). Both definitions of urban elite (with or without the SLI criterion) give almost identical results. We therefore estimate Model 6 for the group WBELITE′ = 1, incorporating preferences about family size and gender composition through the variable gender parity (SEXCOMP). Thus, the model estimated is as follows:

$$RV313 = \alpha + \beta_1\, V012 + \beta_2\, SV012 + \beta_3\, P\_PRIMARY + \beta_4\, P\_SECONDARY + \beta_5\, HSC + \beta_6\, HST + \beta_7\, MUSLIM + \beta 8\, OTHERS + \beta_9\, LCHILD + \beta_{10}\, NFHS2 + \beta_{11}\, NFHS3 + \beta_{12}\, SEXCOMP1 + \beta_{13}\, SEXCOMP2 + \beta_{14}\, SEXCOMP4 + \beta_{15}\, SEXCOMP5 + \beta_{16}\, SEXCOMP6 + u_i \quad [6]$$

when,

SEXCOMP1: Gender parity (0, 0)
SEXCOMP2: Gender parity (1, 0)
SEXCOMP4: Gender parity (2, 0)
SEXCOMP5: Gender parity (2, 1)
SEXCOMP6: Higher order gender parity
(reference category) SEXCOMP3: Gender parity (1, 1)

Results are stated in Table 3.7.

It can be seen that preference for behavioural family planning methods increases as respondents become older, though the relation is nonlinear.[16] Occupation of partner does not appear to be relevant;[17] nor is number of living child. Over time, preference for behavioural methods of birth control seems to be increasing among urban elites, though preference for behavioural methods and modern methods tapers off around 2005–2006 (NFHS-3). Socio-religious identity is not relevant—the RRR of only MUSLIM is significant at 5 % level and greater than unity. While this may be cited as support for the claim that Muslims have an aversion towards using contraceptive methods, two riders should be noted. Firstly, the sample is urban elite —a group that is a minority within Muslims (comprising only 5 % within West Bengal Muslim community, which is less than the population share of HSC, HFC, and Others).

The variables in which we are most interested in are the dummy variables SEXCOMP1-SEXCOMP6. The reference category was SEXCOMP3, corresponding to a family with one son and one daughter. RRR's of families in the immediate neighbourhood (SEXCOMP2 and SEXCOMP4) are not statistically significant. What is interesting is that coefficient of SEXCOMP1 is negative and significant at 5 % level, and that of SEXCOMP5 and SEXCOMP6 are also significant at 5 % level, but positive. *This implies that childless couples (SEXCOMP0)*

[16]This may reflect declining sexual activity with age. The infrequent intervals at which sexual activity occur—the suddenness and unpremeditated nature of the act—means that women have to rely on methods that can be employed without the need for prior preparation. This may create a preference for traditional methods such as *coitus interruptus*.

[17]Women whose partners are engaged in primary sector display a weak preference towards traditional methods over modern methods, in comparison with women having unemployed partners. This effect is significant at 10 % level.

Table 3.7 Regression results for currently married urban elite in West Bengal

RV313	Choice: Folkloric/No use			Choice: Modern methods		
	RRR	Z	Prob.	RRR	z	Prob.
V012	0.42	−10.40***	0.00	0.73	−4.46***	0.00
SV012	1.01	10.78***	0.00	1.00	3.64***	0.00
PRIMARY_P	1.32	0.71	0.48	0.61	−1.71*	0.09
SECONDARY_P	1.44	1.02	0.31	0.70	−1.32	0.19
HSC	0.76	−0.95	0.34	1.01	0.04	0.97
HST	0.00	0.00	1.00	0.58	−0.54	0.59
MUSLIM	1.92	2.17**	0.03	0.91	−0.37	0.71
OTHER	0.65	−0.72	0.47	1.22	0.54	0.59
V218	1.32	1.04	0.30	1.18	0.77	0.44
NFHS2	0.19	−2.67**	0.01	0.35	−1.84**	0.07
NFHS3	0.18	−2.69**	0.01	0.46	−1.36	0.17
RSEXCOMP1	1.06	0.15	0.88	0.53	−2.00**	0.05
RSEXCOMP2	1.07	0.17	0.87	0.77	−0.83	0.41
RSEXCOMP4	1.12	0.38	0.71	1.43	1.51	0.13
RSEXCOMP5	0.68	−1.02	0.31	1.73	2.05**	0.04
RSEXCOMP6	0.66	−0.79	0.43	2.77	2.54**	0.01
N	**1688.00**					
LR χ^2	**343.11**		**0.00**			
PSEUDO R^2	**0.10**					

Note
[1] *Choice 0* "Not using any contraceptives, or using folkloric methods"; *Choice 2* "using modern contraceptive methods"; Base outcome (*Choice 1*) "Using behavioural contraceptive method"
[2] ***denotes $p < 0.01$, **denotes $p < 0.05$, and *denotes $p < 0.10$

prefer traditional methods over modern methods, while this choice gets reversed for families with higher parity (SEXCOMP5 SEXCOMP6). Multivariate analysis of choice of contraceptive method provides evidence that the preference of "ultra-modern contraception" is linked to son preference, which has traditionally been observed to guide fertility decisions in South Asia (Arnold et al. 1998; Arnold 2001; Clark 2000; Das Gupta et al. 2003; Dutta and Husain 2011; Jayaraman et al. 2009; Pande 2003; Stash 1996).

3.7 Limitations of NFHS-Based Analysis

While our analysis of NFHS data in this chapter had provided a useful introduction to the problem, as well as refuting the "ultra-modern" contraception hypothesis, it has some limitations, mainly NFHS collects information only about current use and ever use. Further, respondents are allowed to identify only one contraception method. This approach may be justified on practical grounds—namely, that the survey also collects a host of other information—but it overlooks certain facts. Firstly, surveys of contraception use report that women frequently combine more than one method; further, depending upon their life cycle and gender reproductive history, they may also switch from one contraception method to another. It was with this objective that we undertook a primary survey of currently married graduate women from Kolkata. Results of the analysis from the primary survey are discussed in the subsequent chapters.

References

Arnold, F., Choe, M. K., & Roy, T. K. (1998). Son preference, the family-building process and child mortality in India. *Population Studies, 52*(3), 301–315.

Arnold, F. (2001). Son preference in South Asia. In Z. A. Sathar & J. F. Phillips (Eds.), *Fertility transition in South Asia*. Clarendon: Oxford University Press.

Basu, A. M. (2005). Ultramodern contraception: Social class and family planning in India. *Asian Population Studies, 1*(3), 303–323.

Bledsoe, C. (1996). Contraception and "Natural" Fertility in America. *Population and Development Review 22* (pp. 297–324), Supplement: Fertility in the United States: New Patterns, New Theories.

Castiglioni, M., Dalla Zuanna, G., & Loghi, M. (2001). Planned and unplanned births and conceptions in Italy, 1970–1995. *European Journal of Population, 17*(3), 207–233.

Clark, S. (2000). Son preference and sex decomposition of children: Evidence from India. *Demography, 37*(1), 95–108.

Dalla Zuanna, G., De Rose, A., & Racioppi, F. (2005). Low fertility and limited diffusion of modern contraception in Italy during the second half of the twentieth century. *Journal of Population Research, 22*, 21–48.

Das Gupta, M., Zhenghua, J., Bohua, L., Zhenming, X., Chung, W., & Hwa-ok, B. (2003). Why is son preference so persistent in East and South Asia? A cross-country study of China, India and the Republic of Korea. *The Journal of Development Studies, 40*(2), 153–187.

Dude, A., Neustadt, A., Martin, S., & Gilliam, M. (2013). Use of withdrawal and unintended pregnancy among females 15–24 years of age. *Obstetrics Gynecology, 122*(3), 595–600.

Dutta, M., & Husain, Z. (2011). Balancing the present and future: A study of contraceptive use in Calcutta's slums. *World Health and Population, 12*(3), 23–32.

Elmendorf, M. (1979). Anita: A Mayan peasant woman copes. *Studies in Family Planning, 10* (11/12), 418–420.

Erfani, A., & Yuksel-Kaptanoglu, I. (2012). The use of withdrawal among birth limiters in Iran and Turkey. *Studies in Family Planning, 43*, 21–32.

Fisher, K. (2000). Uncertain aims and tacit negotiation: Birth control practices in Britain 1925-1950. *Population Development Review, 26*, 295–317.

Flandrin, J. L. (1979). *Families in former times: Kinship, household and sexuality*. New York: Cambridge University Press.

Georges, E. (1996). Abortion policy and practice in Greece. *Social Science Medicine, 42*(4), 509–519.

Giacobazzi, D., Merelli, M., Morini, M., Nava, P., & Ruggerini, M. (1989). *I Percorsi del Cambiamen to. Ricerca sui Comportamenti Contraccettivi in Emilia Romagna*. Torino: Rosenberg e Sellier.

Gray, A., Chowdhury, J. H., Caldwell, B., & Al-Sabir, A. (1997). *Traditional' family planning in Bangladesh*. Dhaka: Population Council.

Gribaldo, A., Judd, M. D., & Kertzer, D. I. (2009). An imperfect contraceptive society: Fertility and contraception in Italy. *Population Development Review, 35*, 551–584.

Husain, Z., Ghosh, S., & Dutta, M. (2013). 'Ultramodern Contraception' Re-Examined, *Asian Population Studies, 9*(3), 280–300. doi: 10.1080/17441730.2013.816480

Jayaraman, A., Mishra, V., & Arnold, F. (2009). The relationship of family size and composition to fertility desires, contraceptive adoption and method choice in South Asia. *International Perspectives on Sexual and Reproductive Health, 35*(1), 29–38.

Jha, P., Kesler, M. A., Kumar, R., Ram, F., Ram, U. L., Aleksandrowicza, L., et al. (2011). Trends in selective abortions of daughters in India: analysis of nationally representative birth histories from 1990 to 2005 and census data from 1991 to 2011. *Lancet, 377*(781), 1921–1928.

Johnson-Hanks, J. (2002). On the modernity of traditional contraception: Time and the social context of fertility. *Population and Development Review, 28*(2), 229–249.

Johnson-Hanks, J. (2005). When the future decides: Uncertainty and intentional action in Contemporary Cameroon. *Current Anthropology, 46*(3), 363–385.

Juarez, F., Cabigon, J., & Singh, S. (2009). High prevalence of traditional methods and unwanted pregnancies: Barriers to obtaining family planning services in the Philippines. *Paper presented in Population Association of America 2009 Annual Meeting*, Detroit, Michigan, April 30–May 2. http://paa2009.princeton.edu/download.aspx?submissionId=90756. Accessed July 15, 2011.

Krause, E. (2005). A crisis of births: Population politics and family making in Italy. Thomson/Wadsworth: Belmont, CA.

Loizos, P., & Papataxiarchis, E. (1991). Gender, sexuality, and the person in Greek culture. In P. Loizos Papataxiarchis (Ed.), *Contested identities: Gender and kinship in modern Greece*. Princeton: Princeton University Press.

McLaren, A. (1990). *A History of contraception: From antiquity to the present day*. Oxford: Basil Blackwell.

Mukherjee, S. (2009). Abortion as a process of birth limiting rather spacing among the traditional method of contraceptive users in West Bengal. *Paper presented in 26th International seminar of International Union for Scientific Studies in Population*, Marrakech, Morocco, September 27–October 2.

Nanda, A., & Véron, J. (2005). Child sex ratio imbalances, fertility behaviour and development in India: Recent evidence from Haryana and Punjab. In I. Attańe & J. Véron (Eds.), *Gender discrimination among young children in Asia*. French Institute of Pondicherry: Pondicherry.

Nashid, K., Unnati, R., Saha, M. A. K., & Radheshyam, B. (2007). Use of periodic abstinence in Bangladesh: Do they really understand? *Journal of Biosocial Science, 39*, 27–40.

Nguyen, H. N., & Miller, P. (2012). The use of traditional contraceptive methods in a northern province in Vietnam. *Paper presented in Second Asian Population Conference*, Bangkok, 26–29 August.

Otoide, V. O., Oronsaye, F., & Okonofua, F. E. (2001). Why Nigerian adolescents prefer abortion rather than contraception: Evidence from focus group discussion. *International Family Planning Perspectives, 27*(2), 77–81.

Pande, R. (2003). Selective gender differences in childhood nutrition and immunization in rural India: The role of siblings. *Demography, 40*(3), 318–395.

Petchesky, R. (1990). *Abortion woman's choice: The state, sexuality, and reproductive freedom* (Revised Ed.) Boston: Northeastern University Press.

Puri, J. (1999). *Women, body, desire in post-colonial India*. New York: Routledge.

Ramaswamy, S., & Smith, T. (Eds.). (1976). *Practical contraception*. Tunbridge Wells: Pitman Medical.

Roy, T. K., Jayachandran, V., & Banerjee, S. K. (1999). Economic condition and fertility: Is there a relationship? *Economic and Political Weekly, 3*(42–43), 3041–3046.

Rutenberg, N and S.C. Watkins (1997). The buzz outside the clinics: Conversations an dcontraception in Nyanza Province, kenya, *Studies in Family Planning, 28*(4), 290–307.

Sato, R., & Iwasawa, M. (2006). Contraceptive use and induced abortion in Japan: How is it so unique among the developed countries? *The Japanese Journal of Population, 4*(1), 33–54.

Schneider, J., & Schneider, P. (1991). Sex and respectability in an age of fertility decline: A sicilian case study. *Social Science Medicine, 33*(8), 885–895.
Stash, S. (1996). Ideal family size and sex-composition preferences among husbands and wives of Nepal. *Studies in Family Planning, 7*(2), 107–118.
Schneider, J., & Schneider, P. T. (1996). Festival of the poor: Fertility decline and the ideology of class in Sicily 1860–1980. Tucson: Arizona Press.
Thapan, M. (1997). *Essays on gender and identity*. New Delhi: Oxford University Press.
Uberoi, P., & Bahadur, T. (2001). The woman's body in mid-life: Sociocultural and medical perspectives from South Asia. *Occasional Papers in Sociology* (No. 4), New Delhi: Institute of Economic Growth.

Chapter 4
Current Contraception Use

A Survey of Currently Married Graduates in Kolkata

Abstract This chapter examines whether son preference may be a possible explanation of the reliance on behavioural contraceptive methods based on a primary survey collecting information on current contraception use by currently married graduates residing in Kolkata. The study finds that awareness is still low about contraception methods—with respondents spontaneously reporting that they have heard about condoms and pills. The majority of respondents report current use of behavioural methods and condoms. Withdrawal, in particular, appears to be the most popular method; moreover, reliance on this method increases with age. The main reason for the popularity of withdrawal is that it can be used without prior preparation. The attempt to correlate use of withdrawal and rhythm with gender parity is not very successful and indicates the absence of son preference among educated women in Kolkata. However, users of behavioural methods do not seem to be very successful in using such methods to regulate fertility. Although awareness of "safe" methods is high, loss of control and variations in timing of menstrual cycle has led to method failure. The common recourse in such cases is medical termination of pregnancy (MTP). The health implications of these practices stemming from the failure of contraception methods can be quite serious and needs to be explored in greater details. Finally, a multinomial logit model is estimated to identify determinants of contraception method. The analysis, however, fails to provide evidence in support of the son preference observed in the case of NFHS data. One possible reason is the difference in time periods. We suggest possible reasons why son preference may have dwindled away. The absence of son preference in recent times implies that we have to seek for another explanation of the reliance on behavioural methods.

Keywords Medical termination of pregnancy · Rhythm · Son preference · Withdrawal

Z. Husain and M. Dutta, *Fertility Control in a Risk Society*,
SpringerBriefs in Population Studies, DOI 10.1007/978-81-322-3685-6_4

4.1 Background of the Primary Survey

This chapter discusses current use of contraceptive method based on data collected from the survey of currently married graduates in Kolkata. As mentioned in Chap. 3, the survey covered currently married graduate women in Kolkata. The justification of limiting our sample to graduates is that the hypothesis of "ultramodern" contraception had focussed on the behaviour of graduates. The choice of geographical region was dictated by the high prevalence rate of behavioural method in urban West Bengal, as revealed in the DHS survey.

Apart from questions on the demographic profile, decision-making power and asset holding of the respondent, the survey elicited information about reproductive behaviour in two ways. Firstly, the questionnaire seeks information about awareness about contraception method and birth control method being used currently (exploring reasons for the choice). Thereafter, it focuses behavioural methods, seeking information on issues such as follows:

- Ever use of such methods,
- Reasons for use,
- Satisfaction with such methods,
- Reasons for dissatisfaction,
- Knowledge of ovulation, and
- Incidence of RTI/STI.

In this chapter, we analyse this data. In the first part, we focus on awareness and (current and ever) use. In the second part, we analyse the information on current contraceptive method, motives underlying choice of methods, and determinants of contraception choice.

In addition, using a schedule, we sought information on use of family planning method used at different points of the life cycle. This part of the questionnaire discards the implicit assumption that women use one method at a time; instead, we seek information on the combination of modern and behavioural methods used at each point of time. The analysis of this module of the questionnaire is undertaken in Chap. 5.

4.2 Awareness and Use

4.2.1 Awareness About Contraceptive Methods

Respondents were asked whether they had heard about different contraceptive methods. Initially, the method was mentioned, but not explained. Depending upon their spontaneous response, the method was explained, and respondents were again asked whether they had heard about the method. It may be seen from Fig. 4.1 that

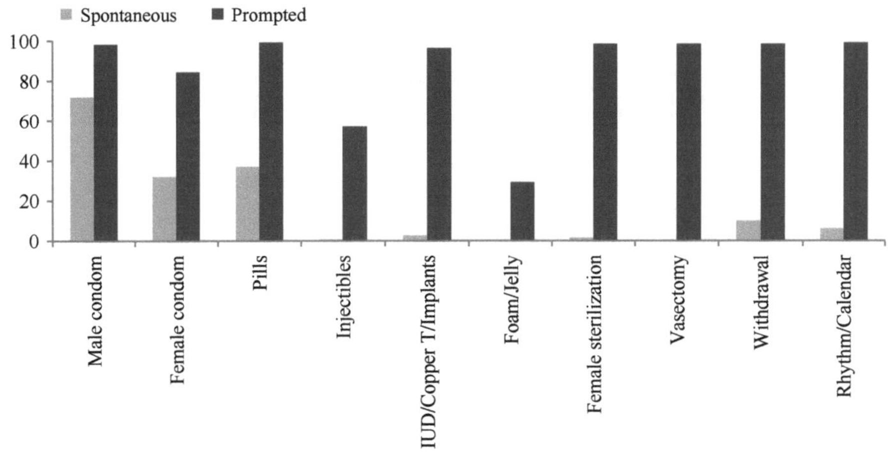

Fig. 4.1 Awareness about contraceptive methods

in general awareness about contraception methods is quite high. Spontaneous responses reveal that respondents are aware about male condoms, female condoms, pills, and behavioural methods. However, awareness about foam/jelly and IUD/Copper T/injectable is comparatively limited.

4.2.2 Use of Contraception Methods

Analysis of responses revealed that 85 % of respondents chose the contraception method jointly; in case of 13 %, the dyad also took medical advice. Only 10 out of 994 respondents had never used a contraceptive. However, when asked about currently use contraception method, this proportion increased to 4 % (Fig. 4.2). Withdrawal is the most commonly used method—44 % of respondents reported using this method—followed by male condoms (22 %) and rhythm (14 %).

The use of withdrawal varies across residential areas (it is more popular among women residing in North Kolkata and Salt Lake), linguistic groups (higher prevalence rate among Bengalis), occupational groups (higher proportion of housewives and businesswomen tend to use withdrawal), and among respondents with lower SLI scores (for all three indices). Variation across religion or caste groups is negligible.

Figure 4.3 indicates that use of condoms and withdrawal are virtually mirror images of each other. While withdrawal-age curve is U-shaped, the condom-age curve is inverse U-shaped; the age group 26–30 years indicates the minimum (maximum) of the two curves.

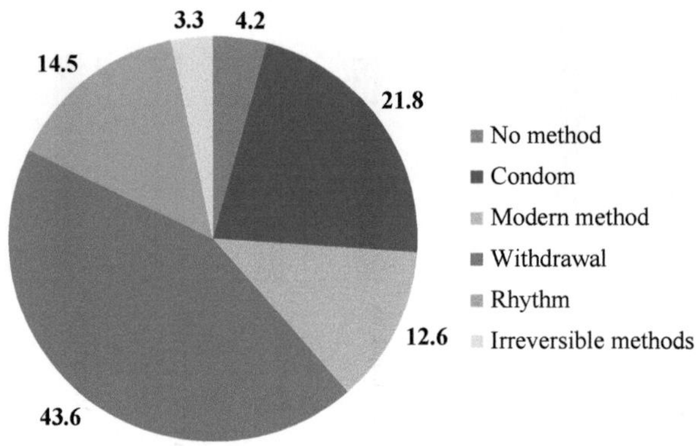

Fig. 4.2 Current contraception use

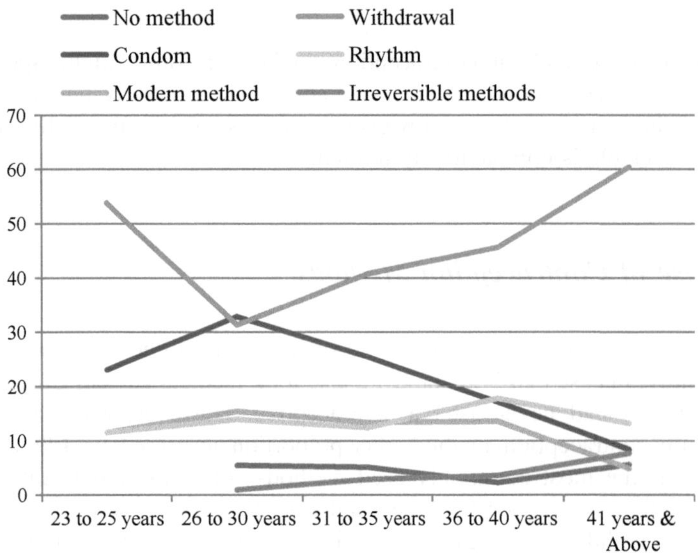

Fig. 4.3 Variations in current contraception used across age groups

The variation in the use of rhythm or calendar method is less substantial. Analysis of responses on current use reveals that Hindus, General castes, and graduates/diploma holders use this method more commonly than other classes.

Table 4.1 presents information on current contraceptive method by gender parity. A high proportion of childless couples uses male condoms; subsequently, the importance of male condoms decline. On the other hand, withdrawal is practised

Table 4.1 Choice of contraceptive method by gender parity

Current contraceptive method	No child	(1 M 0 F)	(0 M 1 F)	(1 M 1 F)	(0 M 2 F)	(1 M 2 F)	Higher birth orders
No method	18.5	1.6	0.9		5.7		
Condom	34.5	19.7	19.7	18.8	17.1		14.6
Modern method	7.1	12.9	15.7	7.8	8.6		19.5
Withdrawal	29.8	46.3	48.9	50.0	40.0	50.0	26.8
Rhythm	10.1	18.9	14.1	6.3	14.3	50.0	7.3
Irreversible methods		0.5	0.6	17.2	14.3		31.7

commonly among all groups but is relatively higher among couples with at least one child. This does not fit in with our initial hypothesis based on the Italian experience, viz. it is the undecided dyads who practise behavioural methods (Fisher 2000; nor does it match the results of analysis of Chap. 4). This implies that the mechanism underlying contraceptive choice among graduate women is different from what was conceptualized both by Basu (2005) and in Husain et al. (2013).[1]

4.2.3 Reasons Underlying Choice of Contraceptive Methods

Analysis of reasons underlying choice of contraceptive method reveals that ease of use is the dominant reason underlying choice of contraceptive (Fig. 4.4). Despite respondent' stating that the decision to use family planning was taken jointly, husband's preference or satisfaction is also given priority when choosing the method. Comfort and reliability are other main reasons.

Investigators also reported a general lack of knowledge and awareness about contraception methods, even among highly educated respondents. Women still adhere to traditional and popular beliefs about the possible effects of modern methods. Concern with real and imagined side effects of methods such as pills and invasive methods often motivated women to rely on behavioural methods—assumed to be without side effects. For instance, some respondents voiced their fears that contraceptive pills would lead to obesity, or that copper T would lead to infections.

Analysis of reasons by age groups provides us with interesting results (Fig. 4.5). As women grow older, they need a method that can be used without prior preparation only during intercourse. In contrast the importance of reliability decreases.

[1]On one hand, Basu (2005) had conceptualized contraception choice as a means of protest against western science and technology and a return back to nature and femininity (discussed in details in Chap. 1). On the other hand, in their critique of this theory, Husain et al. (2013) had argued that the reliance on behavioural methods actually reflects an ambiguous attitude towards fertility control by couples whose son preference had not been satisfied (see Chap. 3 for details).

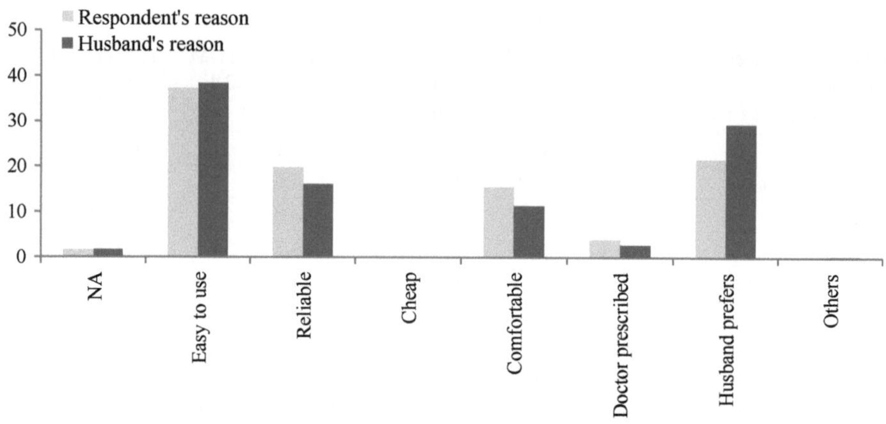

Fig. 4.4 Reasons underlying choice of contraceptive methods

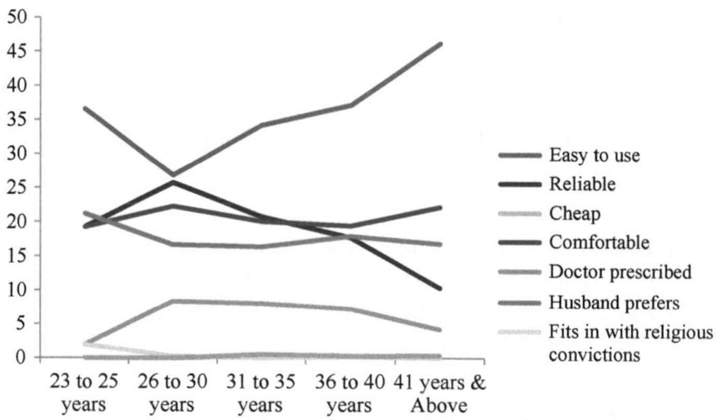

Fig. 4.5 Analysis of reasons underlying contraceptive choice by age group

While the reasons for this change require further investigation, a possible reason may be that the frequency of sexual intercourse declines.

The priority of husband's sexual satisfaction also decreases with age, while the importance accorded to wife's comfort increases. This may reflect the changing roles of women in marital partnerships, with women asserting themselves more in older partnerships.

Another interesting analysis is to see how reasons underlying contraceptive choice vary with gender parity. While easy use (or little preparation) is, by far, the most popular reason underlying contraceptive choice, the importance accorded to satisfaction of husband or comfort of wife decreases as the number of children increases. The importance given to medical advice also increases (Fig. 4.6).

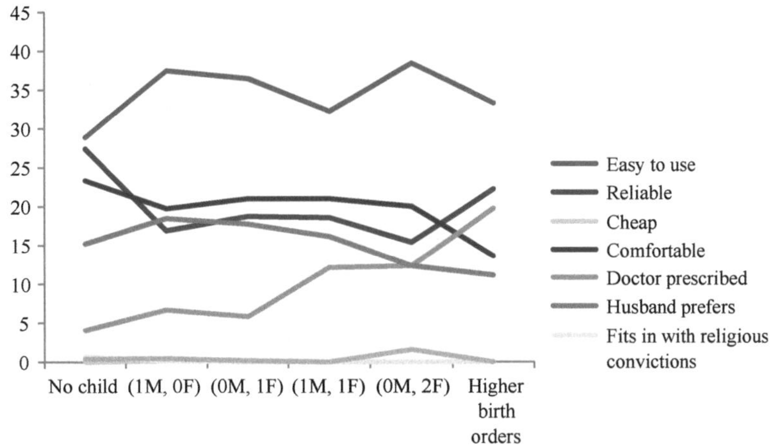

Fig. 4.6 Analysis of reasons underlying contraceptive choice by gender parity

4.3 Use of Behavioural Methods

We now focus on dependence on behavioural methods. From Fig. 4.7, we can see that about 44 % of the sample have used withdrawal frequently, and about a third have used it occasionally (sometimes). The corresponding figures for rhythm, in contrast, are much lower—14 and 8 %, respectively. Only 16 % of women have never practised withdrawal, while 70 % have never used the rhythm method. However, we should keep in mind that the reported use of rhythm may be an understatement as respondents and their partners may not be using the calendar method consciously but have a tendency to avoid "unsafe" periods.

Studies report that women frequently use a combination of coitus dependent contraception methods—practising abstinence during unsafe periods and relying on withdrawal (and/or condoms) during safe periods (Gray et al. 1997, 1999;

Fig. 4.7 Frequency of use of behavioural methods

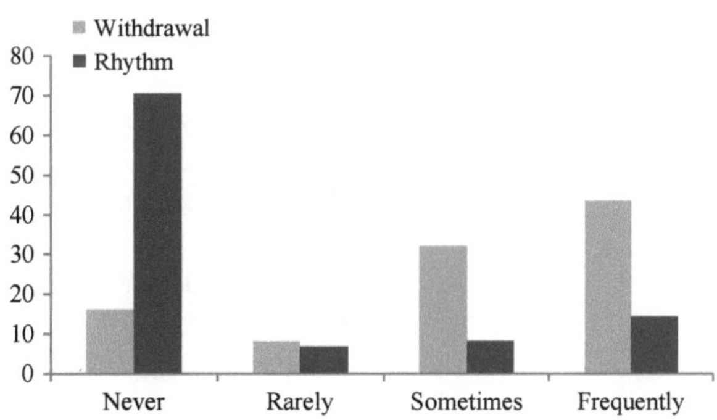

Jones et al. 2009; Mukherjee 2009). Thus, the same women may be alternating between withdrawal and rhythm, depending upon her menses. In contrast, in Kolkata, women generally used either only withdrawal (57 %) or only rhythm (16 %). A negligible proportion (2 %) has used both methods, while one-fourth has not used any of these two methods.

Exploration of the reasons underlying the choice of behavioural methods revealed that ease of use was the main reason why respondents and their husbands preferred these methods. Preference of the husband is also a common reason, while comfort of the woman is also cited. It is interesting to note that respondents do not feel that these methods are reliable; a very low percentage cites reliability as a factor underlying their choice. Further, the rhythm method is considered comparatively more reliable than withdrawal by respondents—8.5 % of rhythm users have attributed their choice to reliability, while the corresponding figure for withdrawal is only 3 %.

Satisfaction levels with behavioural methods are quite high. Only 15 % of women practising withdrawal, and 25 % of women using rhythm express dissatisfaction with these methods. The main reason for such dissatisfaction is fears about their unreliability (Table 4.2). This is a major concern as one out of four husbands has reportedly failed to withdraw in time. In case of rhythm, failure to calculate safe periods is also a major problem. About a third of respondents have reported that withdrawal does not satisfy them sexually.

Given the concern with reliability, the incidence of failure of these two methods is worth estimating. The incidence of unplanned pregnancy is about 17 % in case of withdrawal users and 21 % in case of rhythm users. About 23 % of users of withdrawal reported method failure; a further 8 % were uncertain whether their conception had been due to method failure. The failure rate was 16 % among users of rhythm. In cases of failure, about 53 % took recourse to emergency contraceptives; reliance on medically termination pregnancies was also high (36 %).

A common concern about the use of calendar method is lack of awareness about the ovulation cycle and "safe periods". It has been reported in several studies that respondents often do not know their "safe periods". Given the high level of

Table 4.2 Reasons for dissatisfaction with behavioural methods

Reasons for dissatisfaction	Withdrawal	Rhythm
Not reliable	33.1	45.3
Did not satisfy you	33.9	7.0
Shameful	1.3	1.6
Husband loses control	26.8	8.6
Not healthy	5.0	
Did not calculate safe period properly		36.7
Others		0.8

education and urban background, this proved to be a non-issue as 92 % of users of rhythm were aware of "safe periods". Possibly because of this awareness, the rate of failure is relatively lower in the case of rhythm—only 16 % of respondents report failure. The common recourse is medical termination of pregnancy (MTP) (80 %), followed by medical abortion (11 %). In 4 % (for withdrawal) and 11 % (for rhythm) cases, the respondents did not take any action. The health implications of these practices stemming from the failure of contraception methods can be quite serious and needs to be explored in greater details.

Since behavioural methods imply unprotected intercourse, the incidence of RTI/STI among respondents is also exploring. About one out of seven users of behavioural methods reported having had RTI/STI at some point of time. However, given that the average incidence of RTI/STI is 13 %, the risk of such ailments among behavioural method users does not seem to be very high.

4.4 Current Contraception Choice and Parity

The relationship between parity (number of living children) and current contraception use is examined in Fig. 4.8. It can be seen that as the number of living children increases, the proportion of women not using any method and those using modern method decreases. Reliance on behavioural methods displays an inverse U-shaped curve, peaking for one child. The proportion of respondents using irreversible means is predictably low but increases with parity.

The use of parity has one limitation—it assumes that female and male children are equivalently treated by respondents and their families. This assumption will obviously be violated in societies with son preference. Since we had observed evidence of a weak form of son preference,[2] information about gender, too, should be incorporated into this analysis. In Fig. 4.9, we use the concept of gender parity to overcome this deficiency.

Figure 4.9, however, does not display any tendency to shift from behavioural methods to modern methods after the birth of a son—as observed in the analysis of NFHS data (Chap. 3). The proportion of respondents using modern reversible methods decreases with an increase in gender parity; if one considers modern methods (reversible *and* irreversible methods), then the share of users peak when couples have one son and one daughter—what the majority of respondents have reported to be the ideal combination (Fig. 4.10).

[2]Sons are preferred to daughters, but if two daughters are born then fertility is limited; further no active steps are taken for gender selection.

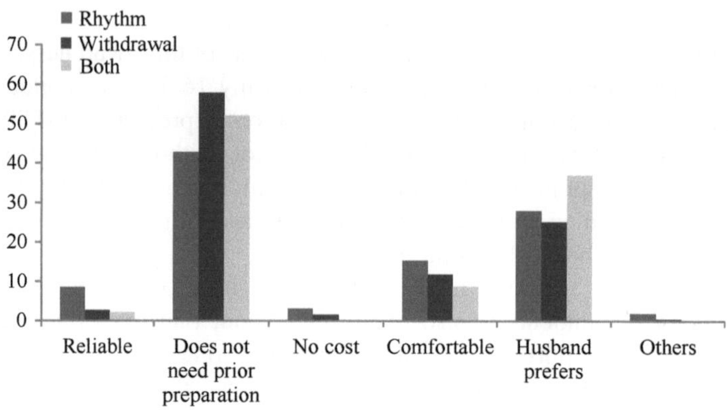

Fig. 4.8 Motives underlying use of behavioural methods

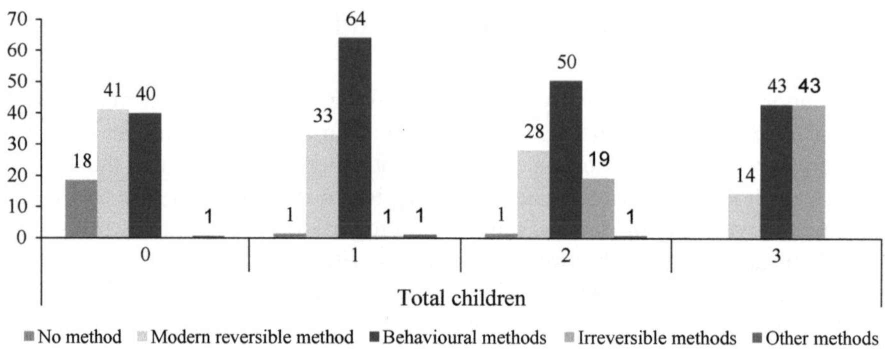

Fig. 4.9 Current contraception method and parity

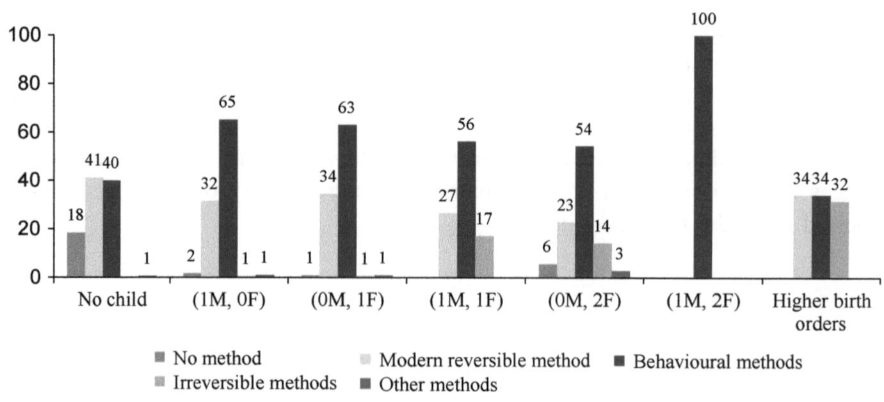

Fig. 4.10 Current contraception method and gender parity

4.5 Econometric Analysis of Current Use

4.5.1 *Models and Their Functional Specifications*

We now turn to an econometric analysis of socio-economic and demographic factors determining current use of contraceptive method. Three models are estimated, with details given in Table 4.3.

The control variables used in the three models are as follows:

- Current age,
- Marital duration,
- Factor analysis scores for empowerment (two indices for financial empowerment and mobility, respectively)
- Factor analysis scores for standard of living (three indices for residential pattern, holiday pattern, and asset holding),
- Religion (Hindu and others),
- Caste (general and others),
- Language (Bengali and others),
- Family structure (nuclear and extended),
- Residential area (North Kolkata, South Kolkata, Salt Lake, and suburban areas of Kolkata),
- Educational qualification of respondent and husband (graduate, postgraduate, professional courses, and postgraduate diploma/certificate), and
- Employment status of respondent (housewife and working).

In models A and B, gender parity (age–sex composition of living children) was incorporated; in model C, gender parity was replaced by number of living children as it gave slightly better results.

4.5.2 *Results of Econometric Models*

In general, we find that, in all the three models, the joint hypothesis ($\beta_1 = \beta_2 = \ldots \beta_m$) is rejected at 5 % level. This indicates that the models used may be used to

Table 4.3 Specifications of econometric models

Model	Choice	Sample	Model
A	Choice between modern and behavioural methods	Users of modern and behavioural methods	Logit model
B	Choice between withdrawal and rhythm methods	Users of behavioural methods	Logit model
C	Sequential choice between: (a) modern and behavioural methods (b) withdrawal and rhythm methods	Users of modern and behavioural methods	Sequential logit

identify the determinants of contraceptive choice. However, when we examine individual regressors, few are found to be statistically significant. In Model A, for instance, we find that respondents married for a longer period, belonging to nuclear families or with lower standard of living (reflected in their asset holding or holidaying pattern) are more likely to use behavioural methods. Respondents with high order gender parity (more than one son and two daughters) are also less likely to use behavioural contraception methods. This may possibly indicate a shift to more reliable modern methods to ensure any further increase in family size (Table 4.4).

Table 4.5 examines determinants of choice between the two behavioural methods. Econometric analysis indicates that rhythm is more popular among women from families who holiday more, among Hindus and among professional women. In contrast, withdrawal is preferred by couples with one son and one daughter.

In model C, the choice process is conceptualized as a two-stage decision-making process. In the first stage, the respondent decides whether to use modern birth control methods or use behavioural methods. After making this choice, the users of behavioural methods have to choose between withdrawal and rhythm.

Results of the first stage model reveals that families with higher asset holding scores and with more living children are more likely to use modern methods. Hindus are found to rely more on behavioural methods, vis-à-vis non-Hindu respondents. In the second stage, we find that Hindu women, those with professional degrees and respondents who holiday more, are more likely to use rhythm (Table 4.6).

4.5.3 Interpreting the Results

Overall, the results of the econometric analysis show that most of the hypothesized variables do not influence the currently used method. There may be several reasons underlying this apparent failure. The first of these explanations is a technical explanation, relating to multicollinearity.

Firstly, some of the variables may be correlated between themselves, leading to the problem of multicollinearity. Most multivariate statistical approaches (factor analysis, MANOVA, cannonical correlation, etc.) involve decomposing a correlation matrix into linear combinations of variables. The linear combinations are chosen so that the first combination has the largest possible variance (subject to some restrictions), the second combination has the next largest variance, subject to being uncorrelated with the first, the third has the largest possible variance, subject to being uncorrelated with the first and second, and so forth. The variance of each of these linear combinations is called an *eigenvalue*. These linear combinations, called *factors*, are used to detect multicollinearity (Belsley et al. 1980).

Table 4.4 Results of logit model of choice between modern and behavioural methods

Variables	Odd Ratio	z	P > |z|
Age	1.03	1.10	0.27
Marital duration	1.04	1.82	0.07
Financial power	1.10	1.20	0.23
Mobility	0.94	−0.75	0.45
SLI1: Residence	1.03	0.38	0.70
SLI2: Holiday	0.85	−2.04	0.04
SLI3: Asset	0.81	−2.22	0.03
Non-Hindu (REF category)			
Hindu	0.78	−0.96	0.34
Backward caste (REF category)			
General caste	1.02	0.08	0.94
Non-Bengali (REF category)			
Bengali	0.81	−0.69	0.49
Extended family (REF category)			
Nuclear family	1.26	1.54	0.12
South Kolkata (REF category)			
North Kolkata	1.33	1.53	0.13
Salt Lake	1.35	0.75	0.45
Suburban	1.05	0.29	0.77
Graduate (REF category)			
Postgraduate	0.83	−0.89	0.37
Professional course	0.89	−0.40	0.69
Diploma	0.74	−1.55	0.12
Working (REF category)			
Housewife	0.92	−0.45	0.65
Graduate: husband (REF category)			
Postgraduate: husband	1.11	0.45	0.65
Professional course: husband	1.13	0.58	0.56
Diploma: husband	1.18	0.60	0.55
Gender parity: one son (REF category)			
Gender parity: no child	1.01	0.05	0.96
Gender parity: 1 daughter	1.17	0.96	0.34
Gender parity: one daughter, one son	0.92	−0.27	0.79
Gender parity: 2 daughters	0.65	−1.13	0.26
Gender parity: 1 son, 2 daughters	0.47	−0.52	0.603
Gender parity: higher order	0.33	−2.85	0.004
Model statistics			
N	952		
LR χ^2	75.93		0.00
Pseudo R^2	0.06		

Note The dependent variable is defined as follows: $y = 0$ implies that respondent is currently using modern contraceptive methods, while $y = 1$ implies that respondent is currently using behavioural contraceptive methods

Table 4.5 Results of probit model of choice between withdrawal and rhythm

Variables	Odd ratio	z	P > |z|
Age	1.01	0.23	0.82
Marital duration	0.98	−0.73	0.46
Financial power	0.42	−1.95	0.05
Mobility	0.70	−0.99	0.32
SLI1: Residence	1.04	0.08	0.94
SLI2: Holiday	1.07	0.60	0.55
SLI3: Asset	0.94	−0.53	0.60
Non-Hindu (REF category)			
Hindu	0.96	−0.38	0.70
Backward caste (REF category)			
General caste	0.79	−2.19	0.03
Non-Bengali (REF category)			
Bengali	1.09	0.70	0.48
Extended family (REF category)			
Nuclear family	1.28	1.22	0.22
South Kolkata (REF category)			
North Kolkata	1.37	1.23	0.22
Salt Lake	1.26	0.41	0.68
Suburban	1.16	0.67	0.50
Graduate (REF category)			
Postgraduate	1.38	0.98	0.33
Professional course	0.49	−1.92	0.06
Diploma	0.66	−1.65	0.10
Working (REF category)			
Housewife	0.85	−0.61	0.54
Graduate: husband (REF category)			
Postgraduate: husband	1.64	1.34	0.18
Professional course: husband	1.22	0.66	0.51
Diploma: husband	1.26	0.65	0.52
Gender parity: one son (REF category)			
Gender parity: no child	1.52	1.35	0.18
Gender parity: 1 daughter	1.21	0.87	0.39
Gender parity: one daughter, one son	3.45	2.20	0.03
Gender parity: 2 daughters	0.72	−0.68	0.49
Gender parity: 1 son, 2 daughters	1.00		
Gender parity: higher order	1.33	0.48	0.63
Model statistics			
N	**721**		
LR χ^2	**36.92**		**0.08**
Pseudo R^2	**0.05**		

Note The dependent variable is defined as follows: $y = 0$ implies that respondent is currently using rhythm, while $y = 1$ implies that respondent is currently using withdrawal

The Belsley approach estimates the condition index of each factor. This is defined as:

$$\mathrm{CI}_i = \sqrt{\frac{\lambda_{\max}}{\lambda_i}}, \text{ when } \lambda \text{ is the eigenvalue of the } i\text{th factor.}$$

If the condition Index is above 30, this indicates the presence of multicollinearity. The factor loadings of the variables for such factors are then examined. If two (or more) variables have a "high" loadings (close to unity), then the variables are said to be correlated.

The results of multicollinearity analysis are given in the Appendix. The highest condition index for each of the first two models is: 37.46 and 37.42, respectively. While this indicates the presence of multicollinearity, examination of the results reveals that only age and marital duration are correlated significantly. Dropping marital duration resolves the problem of multicollinearity, without significantly changing the results. The only change is that age of the respondent becomes significant and positive in Model A.

4.6 Son Preference and Behavioural Methods: A Reassessment

The attempt to explain the reliance on son preference in this chapter is not very successful. In particular, the econometric model does not produce satisfactory results. Neither socio-economic characteristics of the respondents nor son preference is found to determine choice of contraception methods. This twin failure needs explanation.

4.6.1 Explaining the Econometric Results

The first explanation relates to the homogenous nature of the sample selected in the primary survey. Based on the analysis of NFHS data, we had deliberately drawn our sample from a narrow band over the education and standard of living scale. The limiting of our sample to only currently married graduate women from middle-class families reduced variations in the socio-economic characteristics of the sample. In the absence of variations in the socio-economic variables, they can hardly be expected to explain variations in choice of contraception method. Thus, reproductive health decisions appear not to vary over the hypothesized socio-economic and demographic variables.

Secondly, if contraception choice depends upon socio-economic characteristics of respondents and their position in the reproductive life cycle, a homogenous socio-economic sample implies that choice of contraception methods and their mix will vary *over the reproductive life cycle* depending upon the outcome of each conception. Further, given the endogenity involved—with fertility and contraception choice being interrelated with each other (see Fig. 1.2c)—this calls for analysis of method choice over the life cycle of respondents.

The third possible explanation is that we are still focussing on a single method—implicitly assuming that the respondent uses only one method at a time. This ignores the fact that several studies report respondents using more than one method at a time (Gray et al. 1999; Jones et al. 2009; Mukherjee 2009). In West Bengal, a study of 100 women found that respondents were practising the calendar method during safe periods; during unsafe periods, they used a combination of withdrawal and condoms (Mukherjee 2009). Gray et al. (1999) report dependence on a combination of condoms and withdrawal (along with rhythm) among users of coitus dependent methods in Bangladesh; this is also supported by Jones et al. (2009) for American couples. In other words, the focus must be on combination of contraceptive methods, rather than on a single method.

4.6.2 The Singular Absence of Son Preference

In the previous chapter, we had found that desire to have a son, along with ambiguity about regulating fertility, was major underlying factors responsible for the reliance on behavioural methods in West Bengal. Analysis of NFHS data indicated that younger women relied on behavioural methods to regulate fertility before their son preference was satisfied. Once this desire was satisfied, there was a switch in contraception choice, with respondents shifting to more reliable modern methods.

In this chapter, however, this son preference is marked by its absence. We find that newly married women tend to rely on behavioural methods. After conceiving, there is a shift to male condoms. This occurs irrespectively of whether the child is a male or female and is guided by the reliability motive. Over time, however, there is another shift—with respondents switching back to behavioural methods on the grounds that they are more convenient and easy to use. This castes aspersions on the hypothesis extended in Husain et al. (2013). While son preference remains a dominant force underlying fertility regulation in North India, it seems to have been eroded over time in Kolkata, at least.

There are several possible reasons this has occurred, so that son preference is not observed in the primary survey. The first point to note is that there is a substantial time gap between the third round of NFHS (2005–06) and the primary survey (2012–13). Between this period, there has been a significant change in social attitudes, residential patterns, postmarital kinship ties, and female work force participation in Kolkata.

Table 4.6 Results of sequential logit of contraceptive choice

Variables	Modern versus Behavioural			Withdrawal versus Rhythm		
	OR	z	P > |z|	OR	z	P > |z|
Age	1.04	1.46	0.14	1.00	−0.15	0.88
Marital duration	1.02	0.72	0.47	1.02	0.78	0.44
Financial power	0.88	−1.23	0.22	1.01	0.12	0.91
Mobility	0.98	−0.27	0.79	1.01	0.07	0.95
SLI1: residence	0.96	−0.31	0.76	0.93	−0.48	0.63
SLI2: holiday	1.04	0.61	0.54	1.23	2.58	0.01
SLI3: asset	0.85	−2.13	0.03	0.92	−0.97	0.33
No. of living children	0.56	−3.78	0.00	1.10	0.50	0.62
Non-Hindu (REF category)						
Hindu	1.60	1.75	0.08	2.15	1.74	0.08
Backward caste (REF category)						
General caste	0.97	−0.09	0.93	1.41	0.96	0.34
Non-Bengali (REF category)						
Bengali	0.79	−0.73	0.46	1.29	0.59	0.55
Extended family (REF category)						
Nuclear family	1.04	0.23	0.82	0.76	−1.38	0.17
South Kolkata (REF category)						
North Kolkata	1.22	0.98	0.33	0.69	−1.46	0.14
Salt Lake	1.13	0.28	0.78	0.82	−0.35	0.72
Suburban	1.18	0.90	0.37	0.83	−0.86	0.39
Graduate (REF category)						
Postgraduate	1.01	0.02	0.98	0.76	−0.86	0.39
Professional course	1.16	0.47	0.64	2.04	1.95	0.05
Diploma	1.18	0.73	0.46	1.40	1.35	0.18
Working (REF category)						
Housewife	1.10	0.41	0.68	1.10	0.35	0.73
Gradaute: husband (REF category)						
Postgraduate: husband	0.78	−0.95	0.34	0.66	−1.15	0.25
Professional course: husband	0.84	−0.75	0.45	0.90	−0.36	0.72
Diploma: husband	1.36	0.91	0.36	0.81	−0.59	0.56
Intercept	1.63	0.56	0.58	0.06	−2.55	0.01
Model statistics						
N	**958.00**					
LR χ^2	**74.07**		**0.00**			

Note The dependent variable is defined as follows. In panel A, $y = 0$ implies that respondent is currently using modern contraceptive methods, while $y = 1$ implies that respondent is currently using behavioural contraceptive methods. In panel B, $y = 0$ implies that respondent is currently using withdrawal, while $y = 1$ implies that respondent is currently using rhythm

For instance, studies of son preference, female foeticide, and marginal role of women within the family reported in social media and mass entertainment channels have transformed patriarchal social attitudes and led to a questioning of the domination of women by society. This has led to a reassessment of the position of women with an appreciation of their role within the household and greater social recognition of their potential social and cultural functions.

The increasing entry of women into the labour force has also played a major role in this attitudinal transformation. It is not simply that more women work—what is important is the motive underlying work, the sectors in which they work, the importance assigned by women to work and the consequent impact on work-home balance. Husain and Dutta (2013) have shown that the desire to create personal space and carve out autonomy are replacing the traditional supplement family income motive underlying work force participation of women belonging to earlier generations. Simultaneously, increasing education of women is encouraging them to seek employment in high-tech jobs such as in the Information Technology (IT) and IT-Enabled Sector (ITES), or in prestigious and/or high paying jobs in the financial and analytics sector, administrative services, or as professionals. While quite a few of such women are not marrying in order to prioritize their jobs, the work-home balance sought by married working women is also departing from traditional patterns. Working women of earlier generations were able to minimise work-home balance through seeking employment in occupations involving routine operations repeated daily over fixed hours and prioritizing family responsibilities over work and personal ambition (Lahiri-Dutt and Sil 2004), so that there was "no major differences in the domestic lives of employed and unemployed women in relation to household work and child care responsibilities" (Dutta 1999: 74). In contrast, working women in the current generation are seeking to attain a more balanced household-work balance by relying on paid services and shifting to a supervisory role with respect to household chores (Husain and Dutta 2013) and relying on multigenerational ties to ensure quality child care services (Husain and Dutta 2015).

The reliance on grandparents—along with the shift to nuclear families caused by factors such as search for housing space, autonomy, and employment—has an important implication. Unlike earlier generations, the residential pattern is no longer with the husband's parents but as separate entities. This provides room for the women to exercise greater autonomy. Simultaneously, however, the realization that maintaining multigenerational ties are necessary in order to ensure quality child care is leading to deliberate efforts to maintain cordial relations with in-laws on both sides. This is leading to the phenomenon of "living apart but together" (Sokolovsky 2001), permitting the wife to maintain strong relations with her parents also. In fact, with social exigency weakening the social taboos discouraging links between a married woman and her matrimonial home after marriage, working women prefer to seek support from her parents as they are more generally more sympathetic to her work aspirations (Husain and Dutta 2015). The establishment of a *quid pro quo* relationship between the two generations means that the traditional cost–benefit ratio of having a son over a daughter has changed. In earlier times, it was generally the daughter who left her maternal home to set up residence in her matrimonial home. Although there were periodic visits, with at least the major duration of the first conception being spent with her parents, such ties gradually weakened over time as she became more involved with the running of her family. The benefit of having a daughter accrued to the groom's family, creating son preference. This has now changed. While both sons and daughters are likely to leave their matrimonial home in search of higher income and greater living space, it will be the daughters who are more likely to re-establish links with their parents and provide support to them in exchange of child care services provided by grandparents. Daughters, therefore, are a better investment option than sons.

In that case, the hypothesis that unsatisfied son preference is responsible for the reliance on behavioural contraception methods is no longer tenable. We have to turn to other explanations to understand why the urban elite rely on behavioural methods.

In the next two chapters, we will address these deficiencies. We will first turn to an analysis of contraceptive *combination* and examine how it varies over the reproductive life cycle of women. Transition matrices will be used to study the *changes in choice of combination of contraception methods over the reproductive phase of women*. This will be followed by the elaboration of the third explanation underlying contraception choice. Based on the works of sociologists examining how people adjust to the stresses and uncertainties of a globalized society, we will argue that factors such as frequency of intercourse and the conditions in which it takes place will also determine the choice of contraception combination.

Appendix: MultiCollinearity Tests Using Condition Indices

Model A:

	index	_cons	q5	mardur	finemp	mobemp	res	hol	asset	nuclear	rpg	rprof
1	1	.	.	.	.	.	.	.	.	.	.	.
2	1.5	.	.	.	.	.	.	.	.	.	.	.
3	2.02	.	.	.	.	.	.	.	.	.	.	.
4	2.17	.	.	.	.	.	.	.	.	.	.	.
5	2.26	.	.	.	.	.	.	.	.	.	.	.
6	2.33	.	.	.	.	.	.	.	.	.	.	.
7	2.4	.	.	.	.	.	.	.	.	.	.	.
8	2.42	.	.	.	.	.	.	.	.	.	.	.

(continued)

(continued)

	index	_cons	q5	mardur	finemp	mobemp	res	hol	asset	nuclear	rpg	rprof
9	2.45	.	.	.	.	.	.	.	.	.	.	.
10	2.51	.	.	.	.	.	.	.	.	.	.	.
11	2.61	.	.	.	.	.	.	.	.	.	.	.
12	2.67	.	.	.	.	.	.	.	.	.	.	.
13	2.74	.	.	.	.	.	.	.	.	.	.	.
14	2.88	.	.	.	.	.	.	.	.	.	.	.
15	3.01	.	.	.	.	.	.	0.34	.	.	.	.
16	3.45	.	.	.	.	.	.	.	.	.	.	.
17	3.72	.	.	.	.	0.63	.	.	.	.	.	.
18	3.89	.	.	.	.	.	.	.	.	.	.	.
19	3.99	.	.	.	.	.	.	.	0.44	.	.	.
20	4.33	.	.	.	.	.	.	.	.	.	.	.
21	4.6	.	.	.	.	.	.	.	.	.	0.34	.
22	5.04	.	.	.	.	.	.	.	.	0.3	.	.
23	9.02	.	.	0.32	.	.	.	.	.	.	.	.
24	**37.42**	**0.93**	**0.99**	**0.57**	.	.	.	.	.	.	.	.

	rdip	rhw	hpg	hprof	hdip	nk	sl	sub	gp1	gp3	gp4	gp5	gp6
1	.	.	.	.	.	.	.	.	.	.	.	1	.
2	.	.	.	.	.	.	.	.	.	.	.	1.5	.
3	.	.	.	.	.	.	.	.	.	.	.	2.02	.
4	.	.	.	.	.	.	.	.	.	.	.	2.17	.
5	.	.	.	.	.	.	.	.	.	.	.	2.26	.
6	.	.	.	.	.	.	.	.	.	.	.	2.33	.
7	.	.	.	.	.	.	.	.	.	.	.	2.4	.
8	.	.	.	.	.	.	.	.	.	.	.	2.42	.
9	.	.	.	.	.	.	.	.	.	.	.	2.45	.
10	.	.	.	.	.	.	.	.	.	.	.	2.51	.
11	.	.	.	.	.	.	.	.	.	.	.	2.61	.
12	.	.	.	.	.	.	.	.	.	.	.	2.67	.
13	.	.	.	.	0.37	.	.	.	.	.	.	2.74	.
14	.	.	.	.	.	.	.	.	.	.	.	2.88	.
15	.	.	.	.	.	.	.	.	.	.	.	3.01	.
16	.	.	.	.	.	.	.	.	.	.	.	3.45	.
17	.	.	.	.	.	.	.	.	.	.	.	3.72	.
18	.	.	.	.	.	.	.	.	.	.	.	3.89	.
19	.	.	.	.	.	.	.	.	.	.	.	3.99	.
20	.	.	.	.	.	.	.	.	.	.	.	4.33	.
21	.	.	.	.	.	.	.	.	.	.	.	4.6	.
22	.	.	.	.	.	.	.	.	.	.	.	5.04	.
23	.	.	.	.	.	.	.	.	.	.	.	9.02	.
24	.	.	.	.	.	.	.	.	.	.	.	**37.42**	**0.93**

Model B

	index	_cons	q5	mardur	finemp	mobemp	res	hol	asset	nuclear	rpg	rprof
1	1	.	.	.	.	.	.	.	.	.	.	.
2	1.52	.	.	.	.	.	.	.	.	.	.	.
3	2.05	.	.	.	.	.	.	.	.	.	.	.
4	2.15	.	.	.	.	.	.	.	.	.	.	.
5	2.21	.	.	.	.	.	.	.	.	.	.	.
6	2.34	.	.	.	.	.	.	.	.	.	.	.
7	2.37	.	.	.	.	.	.	.	.	.	.	.
8	2.4	.	.	.	.	.	.	.	.	.	.	.
9	2.44	.	.	.	.	.	.	.	.	.	.	.
10	2.45	.	.	.	.	.	.	.	.	.	.	.
11	2.52	.	.	.	.	.	.	.	.	.	.	.
12	2.61	.	.	.	.	.	.	.	.	.	.	.
13	2.69	.	.	.	.	.	.	.	.	.	.	.
14	2.76	.	.	.	.	.	.	.	.	.	.	.
15	2.87	.	.	.	.	.	.	.	.	.	.	.
16	2.96	.	.	.	.	.	.	.	.	.	.	.
17	3.47	.	.	.	.	.	.	.	.	.	.	.
18	3.72	.	.	.	.	0.55	.	.	.	.	.	.
19	3.9	.	.	.	.	.	.	.	.	0.34	.	.
20	4.01	.	.	.	.	.	.	.	0.52	.	.	.
21	4.26	.	.	.	.	.	.	.	.	.	.	.
22	4.45	.	.	.	.	.	.	.	.	.	0.37	.
23	5	.	.	.	.	.	.	.	.	0.31	.	.
24	9.02	.	.	0.31	.	.	.	.	.	.	.	.
25	**38.24**	**0.94**	**0.99**	**0.58**	.	.	.	.	.	.	.	.

	rdip	rhw	hpg	hprof	hdip	nk	sl	sub	gp1	gp3	gp4	gp5	Gp6	gp7
1	.	.	.	.	.	.	.	.	.	.	.	.	.	.
2	.	.	.	.	.	.	.	.	.	.	.	.	.	.
3	.	.	.	.	.	.	.	.	.	.	.	.	.	.
4	.	.	.	.	.	.	.	.	.	.	.	.	.	.
5	.	.	.	.	.	.	.	.	.	.	.	.	.	.
6	.	.	.	.	.	.	.	.	.	.	.	.	.	.
7	.	.	.	.	.	.	.	.	.	.	.	.	.	.
8	.	.	.	.	.	.	.	.	.	.	.	.	0.31	.
9	.	.	.	.	.	.	.	.	.	.	0.4	.	.	.
10	.	.	.	.	.	.	.	.	.	.	.	.	.	.
11	.	.	.	.	.	.	.	.	.	.	.	.	.	.
12	.	.	.	.	.	.	.	.	.	.	.	.	.	.
13	.	.	.	.	.	.	.	.	.	.	.	.	.	.
14	.	.	.	.	.	.	.	.	.	.	.	.	.	.

(continued)

(continued)

	rdip	rhw	hpg	hprof	hdip	nk	sl	sub	gp1	gp3	gp4	gp5	Gp6	gp7
15	.	.	.	.	.	.	.	.	.	.	.	.	.	.
16	.	.	.	.	.	.	.	.	.	.	.	.	.	.
17	.	0.31	.	.	.	.	.	.	.	.	.	.	.	.
18	.	.	.	.	.	.	.	.	.	.	.	.	.	.
19	.	.	.	.	.	.	.	.	.	.	.	.	.	.
20	.	.	.	.	.	.	.	.	.	.	.	.	.	.
21	.	.	.	.	.	.	.	.	.	.	.	.	.	.
22	.	.	.	.	.	.	.	.	.	.	.	.	.	.
23	.	.	.	.	.	.	.	.	.	.	.	.	.	.
24	.	.	.	.	.	.	.	.	.	.	.	.	.	.
25	.	.	.	.	.	.	.	.	.	.	.	.	.	.

References

Basu, A. M. (2005). Ultramodern contraception: Social class and family planning in India. *Asian Population Studies, 1*(3), 303–323.

Belsley, D., Kuh, E., & Welsch, R. (1980). *Regression diagnostics*. New York: Wiley.

Dutta, M. (1999). Gender equality in families: Bengali middle class employed women in India. *Contemporary South-east Asia, 8*(2), 161–176.

Fisher, K. (2000). Uncertain aims and tacit negotiation: Birth control practices in Britain, 1925–50. *Population Development Review, 26*(2), 295–317.

Gray, A., Chowdhury, J. H., Caldwell, B., & Al-Sabir, A. (1997). *Traditional' family planning in Bangladesh*. Dhaka: Population Council.

Gray, A., Chowdhury, J. H., Caldwell, B., & l-Sabir, A. (1999). Coitus-dependent family planning methods: Observations from Bangladesh. *Studies in Family Planning, 30*(1), 43–53.

Husain, Z., Ghosh, S., & Dutta, M. (2013). 'Ultramodern contraception' re-examined: Cultural dissent or son preference? *Asian Population Studies, 9*(3), 280–300.

Husain, Z., & Dutta, M. (2013). *Women in Kolkata's IT sector: Satisficing between work and home*. New Delhi: Springer.

Husain, Z., & Dutta, M. (2015). Grandparental childcare and labour market participation of mothers in India. *Economic and Political Weekly, 50*(21), 74–81.

Jones, R. K., Fennell, J., Higgins, J. A., & Blanchard, K. (2009). Better than nothing or savvy risk-reduction practice? The importance of withdrawal. *Contraception, 79*(6), 407–410.

Lahiri-Dutt, K., & Sil, P. (2004). Beyond the boundary: Middle class women in income generating activities in Burdwan, India. *Contemporary Asia, 13*(3), 257–272.

Mukherjee, S. (2009). Abortion as a process of birth limiting rather spacing among the traditional method of contraceptive users in West Bengal. *Paper presented in 26th International seminar of International Union for Scientific Studies in Population*, Marrakech, Morocco, September 27–October 2.

Sokolovsky, J. (2001). Living arrangements of older persons and family support in less developed countries. *Population Bulletin of the United Nations, Special Issue (Living arrangements of older persons—Critical issues and policy responses), 42/43*, 162–192.

Chapter 5
Method or Methods?

What Happens Over the Lifespan

Abstract Although women generally mix or alternate between contraception methods within short periods, reproductive surveys generally elicit information only on current method used. This implicitly assumes that the respondent uses only one method at a time. In this chapter, we discard this presumption and collect information on the combination of modern and behavioural contraception methods used by the respondents. We analyse how such combinations vary with age and number of conceptions and the reasons underlying their choice. Even this method, however, has a limitation as we cannot distinguish between respondents persistently using the same combination and respondents who shift to other combinations over time. To analyse such shifts, we use the concept of transition matrices. The rows of these matrices depict the methods used in period t, while the columns depict the combinations chosen in period t + 1. Using conceptions, we divide the reproductive life cycle of women into several sequential stages and study how women shift from one combination to another over their reproductive life cycle. This chapter concludes by using a multinomial logit model to determine the factors determining choice of combination of contraception methods.

Keywords Combination of contraception methods · Conceptions · Multinomial logit · Transition matrix

5.1 Analysing Mix of Contraception Methods

We had pointed out that most surveys of contraceptive use have implicitly assumed that respondents use only contraception method at a particular point of time. Hence, such studies record only ever use and current use of contraception methods. This approach overlooks the finding of several microstudies that report that many women use two or more methods in combination:

> "Generally, both demographers and providers have ignored the finding that many women use more than one method; they may mix or alternate methods, sometimes within short

Z. Husain and M. Dutta, *Fertility Control in a Risk Society*,
SpringerBriefs in Population Studies, DOI 10.1007/978-81-322-3685-6_5

periods. Therefore, a woman who takes the pill when she remembers and practices periodic abstinence or withdrawal when she does not may describe herself as a pill user. Even if she reports both methods, her response is still coded according to the most effective method in most studies" (Rogow and Horowitz 1995: 142).

In our survey, we had sought information on the main contraception method applied (and the main reason for its use), along with a question on whether behavioural methods were also used (and why). The information on main contraception method and behavioural method used in conjunction with such method was combined to form a variable indicating the combination of contraception methods. The following combinations were identified (after grouping some of the responses):

(i) no method used,
(ii) only condom,
(iii) condom and behavioural method,
(iv) other modern methods,[1]
(v) other modern methods and behavioural method,
(vi) irreversible method,[2] and
(vii) only behavioural methods.

In this chapter, we analyse the pattern of contraception mix and its variation with outcome of each pregnancy and number of conceptions.

5.2 Pattern of Combination Mix

We found that the highest number of conceptions reported was six; however, this was reported by only one respondent. The number of women reporting five conceptions, too, was very low (six). The frequency is so low that there is no point in analysing such cases. So we analyse only up to the first four conceptions. In the first stage, we consider the period after marriage till either survey date or first conception. This stage is referred to as "between marriage and first conception". All the 994 respondents of the survey either are in this category, or had been in this phase. The second stage consists of the period after the first conception and continuing till date of survey or second conception. The sample gets truncated to 844. We consider the next two stages defined as follows:

- Period after the second conception and continuing till date of survey or third conception and
- Period after the third conception and continuing till date of survey or fourth conception.

[1]Includes pills and invasive methods such as foam/jelly, copper T, and intrauterine device.
[2]Comprising of sterilization and vasectomy.

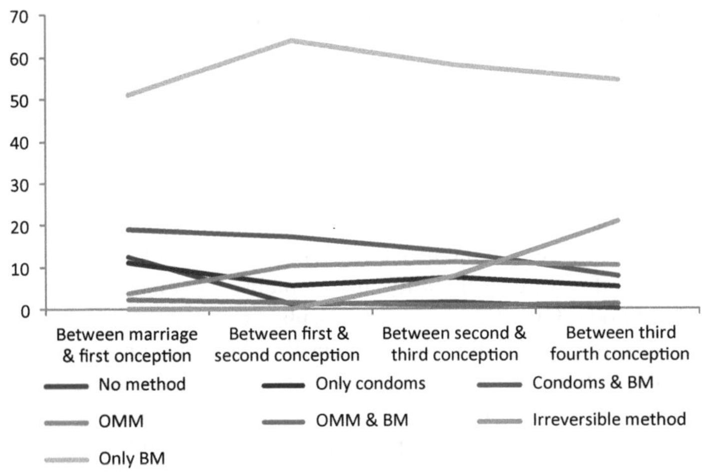

Fig. 5.1 Contraception combination over reproductive life cycle—percent

The number of respondents in each of these two phases is 267 and 77, respectively. Figure 5.1 presents the contraception mix for these cases.

Following marriages, about one out of every ten couples does not use any birth control methods. Subsequently, this proportion falls sharply and becomes nil. The use of only condoms is reported by about 5–11 % respondents, with minor fluctuations. However, condoms and behavioural methods are jointly used by one-fifth of the respondents after marriage; this proportion declines steadily, thereafter. A negligible proportion of respondents report using other modern methods after marriage. Subsequently, this proportion increases sharply and remains steady at around 10 %. In contrast, about 12 % use a combination of other modern and behavioural methods after marriage; thereafter, they shift to other methods/combinations. Irreversible means of contraception are used by women with at least one conception. The proportion of sterilized women increases sharply and steadily till it becomes 20 %. However, the use of this method is not always a deliberate means of birth control but may also be the outcome of the treatment for some gynaecological problem.

Behavioural methods are the most popular contraception method. Over half of the respondents use this method after marriage. After the first conception, this proportion increases sharply to 64 %, before declining gradually. The inverse U-shaped relationship contrasts with other findings linking the age and use of behavioural methods. Goldberg and Toros (1994), for instance, report that the most typical pattern is a U-shaped curve, with the highest prevalence occurring among adolescents and older women.

5.3 Reasons Underlying Contraceptive Choice

During the survey, respondents had been requested to identify the main factor underlying their choice of both main contraception method and behavioural method (if any). Analysis of these responses (Table 5.1) may also throw light on the process of contraception choice.

The majority of condom users cite reliability as the reason for choosing this method. This importance of reliability underlying the adoption of condoms does not change over the life cycle. Reliability also explains the mixture of condoms and behavioural methods. Over 92 % of respondents cite reliability as the main reason for choosing this mix. Reliability also explains the choice of other modern methods, particularly after marriage. About half of the respondents using other modern methods have mentioned reliability as the factor influencing their choice. Subsequently, however, a declining proportion of users of other modern methods cite reliability—22 % (after first conception), 31 % (after second conception), and 22 % after third conception. In contrast, the importance of medical advice rises over the reproductive life cycle—34 % (after marriage), 66 % (after first and second conceptions, respectively), and 77 % (after third conception). Reliability is also the main reason for choosing the contraception mix of other modern and behavioural methods. Irreversible methods, such as sterilization and vasectomy, are not natural choices of respondents—all respondents using this method reported that they had used this method on medical advice.

Finally, coming to behavioural methods, respondents reported that the easiness with which such methods could be used was the main factor dictating their choice of this method. This proportion starts with 92 % (after marriage), rising to 100 % (third conception). Another finding was that just after marriage, 7 % of respondents cited reliability as the reason underlying the use of behavioural methods. However, this percentage declines over the reproductive life cycle.

5.4 Contraception Mix and Pregnancy

5.4.1 Contraceptive Choice and Nature of Pregnancy

The use-effectiveness of behavioural methods is difficult to estimate because data are not available. Out of the eight studies cited by Rogow and Horowitz (1995), most are old and retrospective and have severe methodological weaknesses. These studies report substantial variation in the use of behavioural methods—7 % (Vessey et al. 1982), 10 % (Westoff et al. 1953), 14 % (Kulu-Glasgow et al. 1991), 7 % (Cliquet et al. 1977), 22 % (Peel 1972), and 37 % (Tezcan and Fisek 1983).

Table 5.2 presents the relationship between contraception mix and nature of pregnancy—whether it was planned, whether couples were undecided, and whether

Table 5.1 Reasons underlying the choice of main method over reproductive cycle—percent

Motives underlying the choice of main method	Marriage to first conception					
	Only condom	Condom and BM	Other modern methods	Other modern methods and BM	Only behavioural methods	Irreversible methods
Easy to use	7.3	6.4	15.8	12.5	92.3	0.0
Reliable	92.7	92.6	50.0	70.8	7.3	0.0
Medical advice	0.0	0.5	34.2	16.7	0.0	0.0
Others	0.0	0.5	0.0	0.0	0.4	0.0
Total	110	188	38	24	509	0
	First to second conception					
	Only condom	**Condom and BM**	**Other modern methods**	**Other modern methods and BM**	**Only behavioural methods**	**Irreversible methods**
Easy to use	4.2	6.3	10.5	14.3	95.4	0.0
Reliable	93.8	92.4	22.1	71.4	4.4	0.0
Medical advice	2.1	0.7	66.3	14.3	0.0	100.0
Others	0.0	0.7	1.2	0.0	0.2	0.0
Total	48	144	86	14	540	1
	Second to third conception					
	Only condom	**Condom and BM**	**Other modern methods**	**Other modern methods and BM**	**Only behavioural methods**	**Irreversible methods**
Easy to use	0.0	5.6	3.5	0.0	97.4	0.0
Reliable	95.0	91.7	31.0	100.0	2.6	0.0
Medical advise	5.0	2.8	65.5	0.0	0.0	100.0
Others	0.0	0.0	0.0	0.0	0.0	0.0
Total	20	36	29	2	155	3

(continued)

Table 5.1 (continued)

Motives underlying the choice of main method	Marriage to first conception					
	Only condom	Condom and BM	Other modern methods	Other modern methods and BM	Only behavioural methods	Irreversible methods
	Third to fourth conception					
	Only condom	**Condom and BM**	**Other modern methods**	**Other modern methods and BM**	**Only behavioural methods**	**Irreversible methods**
Easy to use	0.0	0.0	0.0	0.0	100.0	0.0
Reliable	100.0	100.0	22.2	100.0	0.0	0.0
Medical advise	0.0	0.0	77.8	0.0	0.0	100.0
Others	0.0	0.0	0.0	0.0	0.0	0.0
Total	4	6	9	1	42	1

Bold Diagonal elements

Table 5.2 Nature of pregnancy and contraception mix—percent

First conception	Planned	Undecided	Did not want	Total
No use	100.0	0.0	0.0	**123**
Only condom	98.9	1.1	0.0	**91**
Condom and BM	96.6	0.7	2.7	**147**
Other modern methods only	100.0	0.0	0.0	**31**
Other modern methods and BM	85.0	0.0	15.0	**20**
Only behavioural methods	98.4	0.9	0.7	**438**
Total	**834**	**6**	**10**	**844**
Second conception				
No use	100.0	0.0	0.0	**5**
Only condom	86.7	0.0	13.3	**15**
Condom and BM	56.1	3.5	40.4	**57**
Other modern methods only	85.7	0.0	14.3	**14**
Other modern methods and BM	28.6	0.0	71.4	**7**
Only behavioural methods	50.6	3.5	45.9	**172**
Total	**151**	**8**	**111**	**270**
Third conception				
No use	100.0	0.0	0.0	**2**
Only condom	66.7	0.0	33.3	**3**
Condom and BM	42.9	14.3	42.9	**14**
Other modern methods only	100.0	0.0	0.0	**3**
Other modern methods and BM	0.0	0.0	100.0	**1**
Only behavioural methods	52.7	7.3	40.0	**55**
Total	**42**	**6**	**30**	**78**

Bold Diagonal elements

it was unwanted. The proportion of unplanned pregnancies provides a rough estimate of the failure rate.

The first panel reveals that almost all the conceptions were planned. This holds irrespective of contraception mix. One reason for this result may be that the period between marriage and first conception consists of two stages. In the first stage, the main reason for cohabitation is sexual pleasure; subsequently, the motives for cohabitation shift to reproduction. The duration of these periods is not the same for all couples, but may vary with age at marriage, education, and other socio-economic and cultural factors. Unfortunately, given the already sensitive nature of the questionnaire, information on the motivations underlying cohabitation would have been difficult to obtain and may have been unreliable. Hence, such information was not sought. This line of enquiry, however, may be taken up in the future by demographers.

In the second and third conceptions, when the importance of sexual pleasure as the main motive for frequent and regular cohabitation declines, a clearer pattern emerges. Conceptions of all respondents not using any method are planned. Similarly, those *not* using behavioural methods—either singly, or in combination with modern methods—have a high percentage of planned pregnancies. This would imply that couples using such method had shifted to non-use when they had decided to have a child. The failure rate of condoms and other modern methods is quite low—it is about 13 and 33 % (for second and third conceptions, for condoms) and 14 % and nil (for second and third conceptions, for other modern methods).

In contrast, the failure rate of behavioural methods used in isolation, or in combination with other methods, is quite high. For users of condom–behavioural methods mix, the failure rate, measured in terms of unplanned pregnancies, is 3, 40, and 43 % for the first, second, and third conceptions, respectively. Corresponding figures for users of other modern and behavioural method mix are 15, 71, and 100 %, respectively.

The proportion of unplanned conceptions among users of only behavioural methods is negligible after marriage. For subsequent conceptions, however, the proportion of unplanned pregnancies is over 40 %. This finding does not provide support for Basu's argument that users of behavioural methods are highly skilled in their use and can use withdrawal and rhythm effectively to limit fertility (Basu 2005).

Another finding that is at variance with those reported in other studies is with regard to the relationship between spontaneous or undecided pregnancy and use of behavioural methods. It may be recalled that Gribaldo et al. (2009) had reported that many Italian couples were not in favour of planned pregnancies. Their search for spontaneity in sexual relations and reproduction was an important factor underlying reliance on withdrawal. Similarly, middle-class British couples undecided about whether to have a child now or latter also rely on behavioural methods (Fisher 2000; Gribaldo et al. 2009). Our study finds the incidence of undecided pregnancies to be low. Further, such respondents are not, in general, users of behavioural methods. This indicates that respondents of the survey had carefully planned their pregnancies, keeping in mind their social and economic circumstances.

In this context, it may be mentioned that the time gap between marriage and first conception is quite low (2.4 years); this also holds for the time gap between subsequent pregnancies (around 3.3 years[3]). The time gap between conceptions needs to be explored by demographers. In particular, does it vary across geographical regions or over socio-economic stratum? What does the length of the time gap imply?

One possibility is that marriage and womanhood in India is still focused on reproduction—indicated by the social stigma of sterility and childlessness—while cohabitation for the sake of sexual pleasure is still given less importance. In such circumstances, evidence of fertility and the capacity to reproduce need to be produced before eagerly waiting grandparents and other relatives quickly before question arises regarding the virility of the male partner and, in particular, the fertility of the female.

[3]If one deducts the period of pregnancy and lactation, the time gap reduces further.

5.4.2 Outcome of Pregnancy and Contraceptive Choice

Another relationship worth examining is that between outcome of pregnancy and choice of subsequent contraception mix. This is presented in Table 5.3. Outcomes are recorded so that all pregnancies failing to result in a live child are clubbed under the head miscarriages. Thus, miscarriages include medically terminated pregnancies, abortions, miscarriages, and still births.

Irrespective of the outcome, the majority of respondents shift to behavioural methods after the first conception. However, a greater proportion of respondents (about 64 %) adopt behavioural methods if the pregnancy results in a live birth; less than one-fifth use a condom–behavioural method mix, while one out of every ten respondents use only other modern methods. About 57 % of respondents who had miscarriages rely on behavioural methods. The proportion of respondents not using any method is 9 %, using only condoms is 11 % and a combination of condoms and behavioural methods is 13 %.

It is from the second pregnancy that the impact of outcome becomes clear. Among the respondents who have a live son, only 56 % use behavioural methods subsequently. This is much lower than the corresponding figures for women having either a miscarriage (63 %) or a live daughter (70 %). A relatively large proportion of women with a live son rely on condoms (13 %), condom–behavioural method

Table 5.3 Outcome of pregnancy and choice of subsequent contraception mix

Outcome of different conceptions	No use	Only condom	Condom and BM	Other modern methods only	Other modern methods and BM	Only behavioural method
Outcome of first conception						
Termination/ miscarriage	9.4	11.3	13.2	5.7	3.8	56.6
Live son	0.7	5.5	16.9	10.9	1.7	64.4
Live daughter	0.8	5.2	18.1	10.2	1.4	64.3
Outcome of second conception						
Termination/ miscarriage	1.6	7.0	16.4	10.9	0.8	63.3
Live son	1.6	12.5	12.5	15.6	1.6	56.3
Live daughter	1.9	5.6	13.0	9.3	0.0	70.4
Outcome of third conception						
Termination/ miscarriage	5.7	11.4	20.0	2.9	54.3	5.7
Live son	4.8	4.8	4.8	0.0	52.4	33.3
Live daughter	4.8	4.8	4.8	0.0	57.1	28.6

Bold Diagonal elements

mix (13 %), and other modern methods (17 %)—that are more reliable means of limiting fertility than relying only on behavioural methods. The sum of these three figures is 40 %. In contrast, only 34 % of women having a miscarriage and 29 % of women having a live daughter use these methods.

After the third conception, a perceptible "shift" to other modern methods, that are the most reliable methods for limiting fertility, is observed for those with a live child. However, a third of respondents with a live child subsequently use behavioural methods. Among women having a miscarriage in their third conception, subsequently, about a third of such women use either only condoms, or a combination of condoms and behavioural methods, while 54 % rely on other modern methods.

5.4.3 Re-examining Other Modern Methods

The above analysis indicates that other modern methods play an important role in limiting fertility among women with more than two conceptions. In fact, if we return to Fig. 5.1, we will find that after the first conception, other modern methods are more popular than condoms. This motivates us to re-examine other modern methods in some detail. In particular, we try to identify which of the alternative other modern methods is more popular and what is the reason underlying the choice.

Figure 5.2 reveals that condom (alone, or in conjunction with behavioural methods) is a more popular contraception method than pills and invasive methods. However, it may also be seen that over the reproductive life cycle, the importance of condoms declines, while that of the other modern methods increases—till they are equal. Among other modern methods, pills are the most popular. In fact, if we

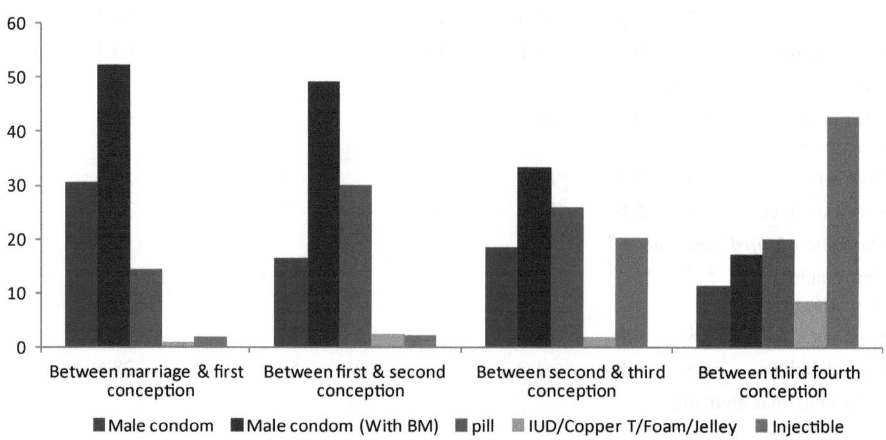

Fig. 5.2 Importance of condoms and other modern methods—percent

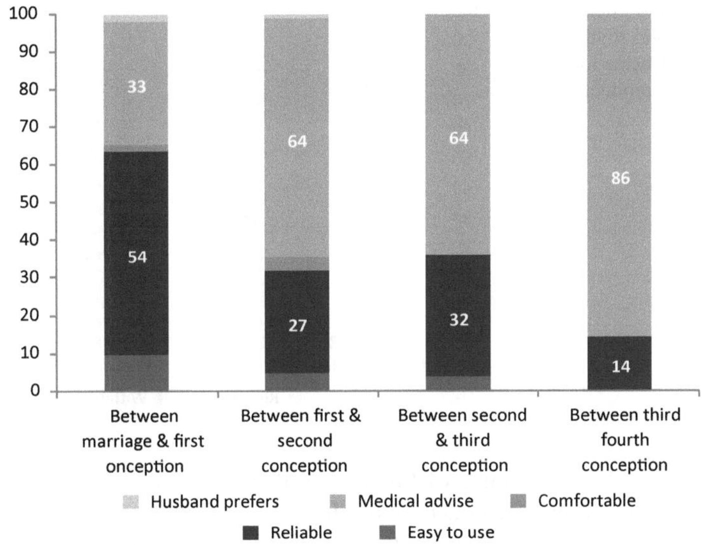

Fig. 5.3 Reasons underlying the choice of pills

consider percentage of respondents using only pills and using only condoms, we find that the former is overtaking the latter in popularity after the first conception.

Investigators reported that immediately after marriage, couples were often unaware about contraception methods and the use of means to terminate possible pregnancies (through emergency contraceptive pills). In such cases, they tended to use condoms as they perceived such methods to be reliable. Subsequently, as they became more experienced, they often took recourse to other means like emergency contraceptive pills. In several instances, some women were reported to use such pills as a substitute for regular contraceptive methods.

Figure 5.3 depicts the reasons for choosing pills. It can be seen that respondents choosing pills are influenced by their reliability. In subsequent stages, however, the importance of reliability declines—we find that medical advice guides respondents in opting for pills.

5.4.4 Rhythm Versus Withdrawal

The relative importance of the two types of behavioural methods also needs analysis. The first point to note is that withdrawal and rhythm are rarely used together—respondents use either (or none) of the two methods. Secondly, withdrawal is easily the more popular method, though its relative importance decreases with the number of conceptions (Fig. 5.4).

The main reason for relying on withdrawal is the ease with which it can be used, without prior preparation. Almost all the respondents practising withdrawal cite this

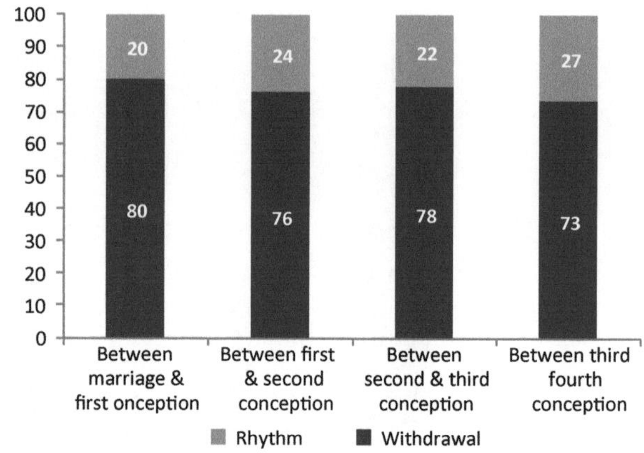

Fig. 5.4 Relative importance of withdrawal and rhythm among users of behavioural methods over reproductive cycle—percent

reason. Further, the importance of this reason does not vary (ranging from 97 to 100 %) with the number of conceptions. In contrast, initially, a fairly large proportion of respondents relying on rhythm cite reliability as motivating their choice. However, this figure declines with the number of conceptions—13, 8 and 5 %, and nil. The explanation that suggests itself readily, and was confirmed in unstructured interviews, is that as women grow older, the ovulatory cycle becomes irregular, so that rhythm looses reliability.

5.5 Transition from One Combination to Another

The analysis undertaken so far is an improvement over the analysis of Chaps. 4 and 5 in that we are allowing for the possibility of method combinations; in addition, the analysis distinguishes between stages of the life cycle using gravida. However, it fails to capture two important aspects. Firstly, the sample is truncated from the second stage onwards as some respondents are dropping out in each stage. Analysis of percentage hides the gradual trimming of sample as respondents with the less number of conceptions do not appear in latter stages. The second problem is that we cannot distinguish between whether one respondent is persistently using the same method and whether she drops out and is replaced by another respondent who was using a different method.

To overcome this deficiency, we use the concept of transition matrices to analyse the variation in contraception mix over different stages. This matrix is constructed as follows. The rows (given by i) denote the contraception mix in the first stage, while the columns (given by j) denote the contraception mix in the succeeding stage. The cell frequency, a_{ij}, will give the number of persons using i contraception mix in the first stage and j mix in the second stage. If there is no change in contraception mix, then we will have only diagonal elements ($a_{ii} > 0$). In reality, however, respondents may change their contraception mix over time. This will lead them to move off the diagonal ($a_{ij} > 0$, $i \neq j$). These absolute numbers may also be converted to transition *probabilities* by taking row percentages.

Tables 5.4, 5.5, and 5.6 present the matrices for transition from marriage to fourth contraception, sequentially. Note that ideally we should have a four-dimension table or graph as there are four stages in the transition. Since this is not possible, we are using two-way tables to depict each transition. The cells denote row percentages—barring the last row and column. These denote the total row and column frequencies. For ready reference, the diagonal elements are given in bold.

It should also be pointed out that at each stage, the sample gets truncated. For instance, after the first conception, 540 respondents use only behavioural methods. Out of these respondents, only 155 respondents have had further conceptions. Details of only these 155 respondents are captured in the transition matrix capturing the transition from stage 2 to stage 3. Thus, failure to "graduate" to the next stage—by not having any conception—is a major reason for truncation. In addition, if a respondent is sterilized, she drops out as the question of changing method will not arise for such women.

Table 5.4 reveals that after their first contraception, respondents not using any method adopt some birth control methods. Interestingly, more than half adopt behavioural methods. In contrast, condom users tend to continue using condoms, but 27 % also start using behavioural methods. The frequency of respondents using other modern and behavioural methods is low (only 20); half discard other modern

Table 5.4 Transition from before first conception to after first conception

After first conception Before first conception	No use	Only condom	Condom and BM	Other modern methods only	Other modern methods and BM	Only behavioural methods	Irreversible	Total
No use	**7.32**	2.44	17.89	15.45	3.25	53.66	0	**123**
Only condom	0	**47.19**	26.97	12.36	1.12	11.24	1.12	**89**
Condom and behavioural methods	0	1.39	**64.58**	6.94	0.69	26.39	0	**144**
Other modern methods only	0	0	6.45	**61.29**	3.23	29.03	0	**31**
Other modern methods and behavioural methods	0	0	0	20	**30**	50	0	**20**
Only behavioural methods	0.46	0.23	0.69	5.26	0.23	**93.14**	0	**437**
Irreversible	0	0	0	0	0	0	**0**	**0**
Total	**11**	**48**	**144**	**86**	**14**	**540**	**1**	**844**

Bold Diagonal elements

Table 5.5 Transition from before second conception to after second conception

After second conception Before second conception	No use	Only condom	Condom and BM	Other modern methods only	Other modern methods and BM	Only behavioural methods	Irreversible	Total
No use	**40**	0	0	20	0	40	0	**5**
Only condom	0	**80**	0	13.33	0	0	6.67	**15**
Condom and behavioural methods	0	12.5	**58.93**	10.71	0	12.5	5.36	**56**
Other modern methods only	14.29	7.14	0	**50**	7.14	7.14	14.29	**14**
Other modern methods and behavioural methods	0	0	0	28.57	**14.29**	57.14	0	**7**
Only behavioural methods	0	0	1.76	6.47	0	**82.94**	8.82	**170**
Irreversible	0	0	0	0	0	0	**0**	**0**
Total	**4**	**20**	**36**	**29**	**2**	**155**	**21**	**267**

Bold Diagonal elements

Table 5.6 Transition from before third conception to after third conception

After third conception Before third conception	No use	Only condom	Condom and BM	Other modern methods only	Other modern methods and BM	Only behavioural methods	Irreversible	Total
No use	**0**	50	0	0	0	50	0	**2**
Only condom	0	**33.33**	0	66.67	0	0	0	**3**
Condom and behavioural methods	0	7.69	**46.15**	15.38	0	7.69	23.08	**13**
Other modern methods only	0	0	0	**0**	0	0	100	**3**
Other modern methods and behavioural methods	0	0	0	0	**0**	100	0	**1**
Only behavioural methods	0	1.82	0	9.09	1.82	**70.91**	16.36	**55**
Irreversible	0	0	0	0	0	0	**0**	**0**
Total	**0**	**4**	**6**	**9**	**1**	**42**	**15**	**77**

Bold Diagonal elements

methods and shift to using only behavioural methods. The use of the condom–behavioural method mix and only behavioural methods is more stable—the probabilities of the diagonal cells are 65 and 93 %, respectively. Although the use of other modern methods is less popular—they are used by only 31 respondents—it is also stable. The value of the diagonal cell is 61 %. In the case of both condom–behavioural method mix and solely other modern methods, 26–29 % of respondents, respectively, are observed to shift to behavioural methods. Overall, the general picture is that after the first conception, a large proportion of women shift to behavioural methods.

In Table 5.5, truncation, owing to respondents being sterilized or not having further conceptions, prunes the sample size down to 267. This reduces the row totals for some combinations—such as no method and other modern–behavioural method combination—so that analysis of these rows may become misleading. The largest row aggregate is for users of behavioural methods. In line with the earlier stage, most of such users (83 %) persist with behavioural methods even after their second conception. Those *changing* methods shift to other modern methods, singly or in combination with behavioural methods.

Table 5.6 has to be analysed with some caution as the sample size falls to only 77. Some row totals are so small that they may be misleading. We find that most of the respondents in this category use behavioural methods. Further, 70 % of such women had been using behavioural methods in the preceding phase. Another important point is the growing importance of sterilization—probably due to gynaecological reasons.

5.6 An Econometric Analysis

Finally, we have estimated an econometric model to identify the determinants of contraception combination and how it changes after each conception. As the choice is between:

(i) no method used,
(ii) only condom,
(iii) condom and behavioural method,
(iv) other modern methods,
(v) other modern methods and behavioural method, and
(vi) only behavioural methods,

we have to use a multinomial logit. Sterilization was dropped as our analysis indicates that it is not a spontaneous decision of the couple, but generally a response to gynaecological problem. Now, this model is based on the assumption of independence of irrelevant alternatives (IIA) (see Chap. 3). This assumption was tested using the test suggested by Small and Hsiao (1985). The results are given in Table 5.7.

Table 5.7 Results for Small–Hsiao test for assumption of IIA

Omitted	lnL (full)	lnL (omit)	chi2	Df	P > chi2	Remarks
Only condom	−587.7	−273.9	627.5	60	0.0	Assumption of IIA violated
Condom and behavioural method	−532.7	−220.3	624.9	60	0.0	
Invasive method only	−461.8	−348.9	225.9	60	0.0	
Invasive and behavioural method	−608.8	−387.5	442.5	60	0.0	

It can be seen that the assumption of IIA is not satisfied. This calls for combination of some of the alternatives. Using the likelihood ratio (LR) test for combining the contraception combinations, we recombine the contraception mix as:

- no method used,
- modern methods only (combining other condoms and modern methods),
- modern and behavioural methods, and
- only behavioural methods.

The reported model (see Table 5.8) is estimated for these alternatives, and the Small–Hsiao test rerun. This time the model is found to satisfy the IIA assumption.

We first examine the results of the top panel. This presents the results for the choice between no method and behavioural methods up to the second conception. Results of the econometric model indicate that as marital duration increases, women are more likely to shift from not using any method to using behavioural methods. Mobile women are also more likely to use behavioural methods after their marriage, though the impact of mobility becomes insignificant after the first conception. The standard of living (SLI) indices are also important after marriage. Women with higher scores for holiday pattern or asset holding, and women with lower scores for residence, are more likely to use behavioural methods. Diploma-holding women are more likely to use behavioural methods after their marriage; in contrast, women with professional qualifications are less likely to use behavioural methods after their first conception. The probability of using behavioural methods is higher among housewives, but only before their first conception. This also holds for women with professional husbands and residing in North Kolkata. In case the first conception results in a live birth, women are likely to shift from not using any method to using behavioural methods. This effect is stronger if the outcome is a male child, vis-a-vis a female child. However, the second conception does not have any impact.

The second panel presents results for the choice of only modern methods versus behavioural methods. Once again, a longer marital duration is found to increase the probability of using behavioural methods. Such methods are, however, less popular among the more affluent respondents, measured by the holiday SLI index (in all three phases) and asset holding SLI index (before the first conception). If either the respondent or her spouse is a diploma/certificate holder, then this raises the

Table 5.8 Results of multinomial logit of determinants of contraception mixture

Variables	After marriage		After first conception		After second conception	
	RRR	z	RRR	z	RRR	z
Model 1: no use versus behavioural method only (Ref category)						
Marital duration	0.97	−2.14**	0.88	−2.31**	0.71	−2.12**
Financial empowerment	0.96	−0.40	1.08	0.21	2.72	1.26
Mobility	0.71	−2.62***	0.62	−1.01	0.27	−1.29
SLI1: residential type	0.79	−1.96**	0.70	−0.90	0.18	−2.02**
SLI2: holiday pattern	1.43	3.26***	1.15	0.37	6.05	1.76*
SLI3: asset holding	1.26	1.79*	0.61	−0.96	1.03	0.03
Family structure: joint family (RC)						
Nuclear family	0.74	−1.46	1.37	0.47	1.28	0.19
Respondent's education: graduate (RC)						
Postgraduate	0.68	−1.29	0.42	−0.67	5.83	1.03
Professional	0.64	−1.05	7.67	1.92**	0.00	0.00
Diploma/certificate	0.60	−1.93**	0.71	−0.38	2.95	0.62
Employment status of respondent: employed (RC)						
Housewife	0.62	−1.80*	0.53	−0.78	0.13	−1.35
Spouse's education: graduate (RC)						
Postgraduate	0.68	−1.03	1.62	0.39	0.00	−0.01
Professional	0.57	−1.73*	0.00	−0.02	0.00	−0.01
Diploma/certificate	0.61	−1.20	0.37	−0.79	1.29	0.14
Residential area: South Kolkata (RC)						
North Kolkata	0.48	−2.90***	0.19	−1.37	0.00	−0.01
Salt lake	0.60	−0.90	0.69	−0.25	66.82	1.69
Suburban Kolkata	0.72	−1.56	2.00	0.94	0.09	−1.59
Last conception: daughter			0.03	−4.61***	0.71	−0.14
Last conception: son			0.03	−4.77***	0.51	−0.46
Model 2: Modern method versus behavioural method only (Ref category)						
Marital duration	0.93	−4.82***	0.94	−3.54***	0.91	−3.67***
Financial empowerment	0.93	−0.67	0.98	−0.16	0.88	−0.58
Mobility	0.93	−0.66	0.98	−0.16	1.01	0.05
SLI1: residential type	0.91	−0.77	1.11	0.83	0.73	−1.35
SLI2: holiday pattern	1.50	3.81***	1.47	3.52***	1.58	2.19**
SLI3: asset holding	1.31	2.12**	1.17	1.19	1.53	1.82*

(continued)

Table 5.8 (continued)

Variables	After marriage		After first conception		After second conception	
	RRR	z	RRR	z	RRR	z
Family structure: joint family (RC)						
Nuclear family	1.09	0.45	0.77	−1.24	1.25	0.56
Respondent's education: graduate (RC)						
Postgraduate	0.86	−0.55	1.20	0.63	3.17	1.97**
Professional	0.65	−1.16	1.23	0.55	0.59	−0.67
Diploma/certificate	0.56	−2.19**	0.86	−0.55	0.72	−0.61
Employment status of respondent: employed (RC)						
Housewife	0.86	−0.57	0.88	−0.45	1.34	0.67
Spouse's education: graduate (RC)						
Postgraduate	1.00	0.00	1.29	0.76	0.50	−0.92
Professional	0.88	−0.46	1.04	0.14	1.95	1.34
Diploma/certificate	0.42	−1.87*	0.57	−1.18	0.39	−1.12
Residential area: South Kolkata (RC)						
North Kolkata	0.54	−2.44**	0.81	−0.82	0.45	−1.52
Salt lake	0.47	−1.28	0.31	−1.47	2.00	0.73
Suburban Kolkata	0.99	−0.04	0.82	−0.84	0.65	−1.04
Last conception: daughter			0.61	−1.75*	0.63	−0.90
Last conception: son			0.65	−1.63*	1.69	1.24
Model 3: Mix of modern and behavioural method versus behavioural method only (Ref category)						
Marital duration	0.93	−5.37***	0.93	−4.51***	0.89	−4.17***
Financial empowerment	0.90	−1.02	0.75	−2.47***	0.95	−0.23
Mobility	1.02	0.22	1.00	−0.02	0.81	−0.83
SLI1: residential type	0.85	−1.60	0.96	−0.36	0.82	−0.82
SLI2: holiday pattern	1.35	3.02***	1.57	4.28***	1.31	1.21
SLI3: asset holding	1.23	1.84*	1.04	0.32	1.22	0.82
Family structure: joint family (RC)						
Nuclear family	0.79	−1.27	0.87	−0.70	1.62	1.14
Respondent's education: graduate (RC)						
Postgraduate	1.30	1.09	1.69	1.96**	4.10	2.32***
Professional	1.14	0.41	0.66	−0.87	0.87	−0.15
Diploma/certificate	0.85	−0.74	1.22	0.80	1.94	1.40
Employment status of respondent: employed (RC)						
Housewife	1.26	1.00	1.13	0.50	1.15	0.30

(continued)

Table 5.8 (continued)

Variables	After marriage		After first conception		After second conception	
	RRR	z	RRR	z	RRR	z
Spouse's education: graduate (RC)						
Postgraduate	1.17	0.57	1.21	0.59	1.10	0.14
Professional	0.76	−1.03	0.80	−0.73	0.98	−0.04
Diploma/certificate	1.10	0.30	0.96	−0.10	0.17	−1.66*
Residential area: South Kolkata (RC)						
North Kolkata	0.93	−0.35	0.90	−0.44	0.73	−0.63
Salt lake	0.69	−0.76	0.72	−0.61	0.63	−0.37
Suburban Kolkata	0.94	−0.30	0.94	−0.26	0.73	−0.72
Last conception: daughter			0.67	−1.51	0.57	−1.10
Last conception: son			0.65	−1.70	0.75	−0.59
Model statistics						
N	994		843		246	
LR χ^2	356.61		406.49		111.07	

Note
1. ***, **, and * denote significance at 1, 5, and 10 % level of significance
2. Choices are no use, only modern methods, modern and behavioural methods, and only behavioural methods (reference category)
3. Assumption of IIA checked using the test suggested by Small–Hsiao and null hypothesis of IIA found to be satisfied

likelihood of using behavioural methods just after marriage. In contrast, post-graduates are more likely to rely on modern methods after the second conception. A successful first pregnancy (irrespective of gender of the child) is again found to increase the chances of the respondent using behavioural methods.

Finally, we consider the choice between the mix of modern and behavioural methods versus only behavioural methods. Marital duration again increases the probability of using behavioural methods. Women who are financially empowered are likely to use a mix of modern and behavioural methods after their second conception. Affluent women, measured in terms of the asset holding index, have higher probability of using the modern–behavioural combination after marriage; higher values of the holiday index have a similar effect, lasting till before the second conception. After their first conception, postgraduates have a lower likelihood of using behavioural methods. In contrast, if the spouse is a diploma/certificate holder, then the respondent is more likely to use behavioural methods.

To sum up, the transition matrices and econometric analysis indicate that there is a natural tendency to drift towards behavioural methods over time. How do we explain this tendency? For this, we turn to the next chapter where we discuss sex in a globalized world and its implications for contraception choice.

References

Basu, A. M. (2005). Ultramodern contraception: Social class and family planning in India. *Asian Population Studies, 1*(3), 303–323.

Cliquet, R., Schoenmaeckers, R., & Klinkenborg, L. (1977). Effectiveness of contraception in Belgium: Results of the second national fertility survey, 1971 (NEOII). *Journal of Biosocial Science, 9*, 403–416.

Fisher, K. (2000). Uncertain aims and tacit negotiation: Birth control practices in Britain 1925–1950. *Population Development Review, 26*, 295–317.

Goldberg, H. I., & Toros, A. (1994). The use of traditional methods of contraception among Turkish couples. *Studies in Family Planning, 25*, 122–128.

Gribaldo, A., Judd, M. D., & Kertzer, D. I. (2009). An imperfect contraceptive society: Fertility and contraception in Italy. *Population Development Review, 35*, 551–584.

Kulu-Glasgow, I., Hancioglu, A., & Akadli-Ergoemen, B. (1991). Contraceptive failure rates in Turkey. *The Turkish Journal of Population Studies, 13*, 3–13.

Peel, J. (1972). The hull family survey. *Journal of Biosocial Science, 4*, 333–346.

Rogow, D., & Horowitz, S. (1995). Withdrawal: A review of the literature and an agenda for research. *Studies in Family Planning, 26*, 140–153.

Small, K. A., & Hsiao, C. (1985). Multinomial logit specification tests. *International Economic Review, 26*(3), 619–627.

Tezcan S., & Fisek N.H. (1983) Epidemiological study: The relationship among contraception, pregnancy and induced abortion. *Acta Reproductiva Turcica October*.

Vessey, M., Lawless, M., & Yeates, D. (1982). Efficacy of different contraceptive methods. *The Lancet, 1*(8276), 841–842.

Westoff, C. F., Lee, H. F., & Whelpton, P. K. (1953). Social and psychological factors affecting fertility. *Milbank Memorial Fund Quarterly, 31*(3), 291–357.

Chapter 6
Contraception in a Risk Society—A New Approach to Studying Reproductive Behaviour

Abstract Globalization has affected social attitudes, norms, and physical environment. While the import of Western ideas and models has led to a relaxation of traditional norms and attitudes governing sexuality, the economic reorganization of society through restructuring of production systems in developing countries has led to the emergence of new forms of stress and uncertainty. This has resulted in the creation of a risk society. Changes in the physical environment—consisting of factors such as long hours, uncertainty in workplace, poor transport system, and rise in temperatures—affect males more strongly, affecting their sexuality. Simultaneously, working place stress and concurrent demands imposed upon working women by the labour market and home influence their fertility decisions as having a child imposes substantial costs on the parents, particularly the women. These factors are hypothesized to influence fertility decisions and contraception choice—rather than standard factors studied in demographic theory and surveys. We conclude by presenting ethnographic evidence in support of our conceptual framework.

Keywords Contraception choice · Ethnography · Globalization · Risk society · Stress · Work-home conflict

6.1 Global Sex

Early theories on globalization viewed this transformation as another phase in the development of capitalism. This view focussed on how the economic requirements of global trade and transnational corporations led to the emergence of a capitalist world system. Dissatisfaction with the overstated economic nature of globalization (in terms of free trade, neoliberalism, financial deregulation, integrated production, and management systems) and the relative neglect of its social, cultural, and political implications led to redefinition of globalization as the interconnectedness of the world as a whole and the corresponding increase in reflexive, global consciousness (Turner 2010).

Z. Husain and M. Dutta, *Fertility Control in a Risk Society*,
SpringerBriefs in Population Studies, DOI 10.1007/978-81-322-3685-6_6

Globalization has not only transformed the world but also revolutionized how we perceive it. Starting with the economic domain, the changes gradually spilled over to the social, cultural, and political spheres. While these changes have been explored by researchers, researchers are only just starting to explore the corresponding changes in sexuality—attitudes towards sex, sexual practices, and reproductive behaviour. Moreover, such studies are mainly undertaken in developed countries, so that there is little understanding of how globalization affects sexual behaviour and reproductive practices in developing countries.

In this chapter, we will discuss how globalization has affected sexual and reproductive behaviour of the urban *middle-class* graduates of Kolkata. The first part of the discussion is theoretical, attempting to lay a conceptual foundation of globalization and sexual behaviour. In the final section, we present ethnographic evidence from our survey in support of the theory.

6.2 Conceptualizing Globalization and Sexuality

Attempts to explain human sexual behaviour and its changes may be grouped into studies focussing on the impact of physical environment, social influences, and cultural forces (Frye et al. 2006). Each of these processes focusses on a particular subset of environmental factors to build up a model of health-related (including sexual) behaviour. The three models are called physical disorder (broken window), social disorganization, and social norms theory. This is summed up in Fig. 6.1.

In the next sections, we briefly examine how globalization influences sexual behaviour using each of these mechanisms.

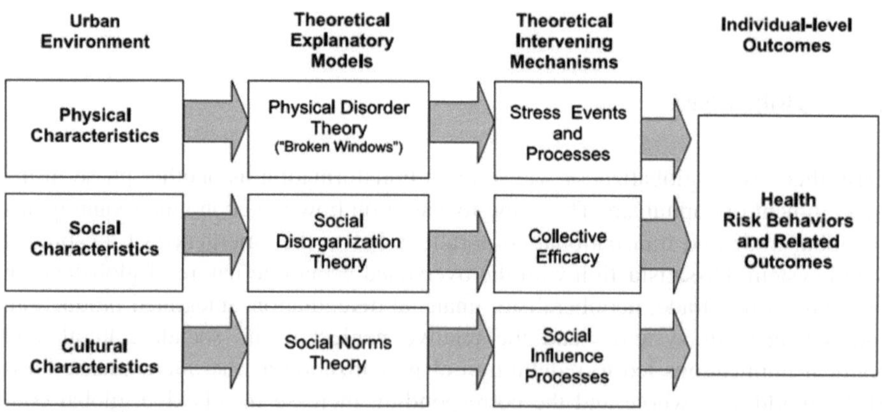

Fig. 6.1 Theoretical linkages between the urban environment and individual health behaviours and related outcomes. *Source* Frye et al. (2006: 310)

6.2.1 *Role of Norms*

The urban social environment in which our sample is located, working and residing, is characterized *inter alia* by cultural norms that define on what type of sexual behaviour is appropriate. They operate at the social network level (operating through the processes of peer effects and diffusion) and at the individual level (through the processes of social learning and internalization of social norms). There is considerable evidence that cultural norms—both actual and perceived—influence sexual behaviour, use of contraception, and choice of methods.

The most importance of the globalized world is perhaps the free flow of ideas and images through the public media and Internet. Altman points out that:

> "As young people pour into the rapidly growing cities across the third world, they are exposed to new media images, through cinema, television, and above all the Internet, which offer radically different ways of imagining sex and gender arrangements and identities (Altman 2004: 64)".

This is remoulding attitudes and social norms towards sexuality, reshaping sexual ethics and establishing new role models in terms of sexual behaviour. The impact of such changes is being reflected in an increased incidence of dating, premarital intimacy (in the form of kissing and smooching) and sex, legitimization of female sexual pleasure, and other sexual practices and ethics (Altman 2001, 2004).

Although such changes are by and large liberating, the composite influence of globalization on sex may, however, be uneven. Altman (2001), for instance, observes that the import of Western attitudes, ethics, and practices relating to sexuality to traditional societies of developing and underdeveloped countries may lead to an emerging conflict between what is global and the local. An example of such conflict in Indian societies is the moral policing of "inappropriate" behaviour imitating "decadent" Westerns by the Hindu ultra-rightists; the attitude of the judiciary towards homosexuality is another example.

6.2.2 *Role of Social Forces*

The economic roots of globalization imply that it is accompanied by urbanization, industrialization, and migration. These disrupt the social structure by affecting the stability in residential pattern, so that the ethnic composition of the neighbourhood may change rapidly. This disrupts the social structure by weakening the social cohesion of neighbourhoods and weakening the ability of social norms and informal social controls to regulate sexual behaviour as it tends to imitate globally accepted practices. Studies of Western societies have observed that such social disorganization can lower the age of sexual debut (Billy et al. 1994; Brewster 1994; Brewster et al. 1993; Crosby et al. 2003; Ramirez-Valles et al. 1998; Upchurch et al. 1999), non-marital intercourse (Brewster et al. 1993; Stack 1994), marital instability (South and Lloyd 1995), and short-term sexual patterning (Browning and Olingen-Wilbon 2003).

6.2.3 Role of Physical Environment

The "broken windows" theory argues that certain aspects of globalization make it more likely that individuals will be subjected to stress and trauma in their daily life. It is not easy to assess the impact of stress on sexuality as "most of the measurable parameters relating to sexual function are influenced by a wide variety of factors, often involving psychosomatic interactions. Such factors include attitudes to sexuality, the effects of previous learning, the quality of the current sexual relationship, as well as physiological mechanisms" (Bancroft 1993: 101). As a consequence, the adverse effects of an environmental factor may be obscured or distorted. While it is difficult to measure the extent to which a specific stress factor affects sexuality, fatigue and psychosocial stress are known to impair sexual relationships, by precluding the optimum circumstances for the expression of normal, healthy sexual feelings. While males are known to be more vulnerable, the impact of stress on the sexual health of women has also been reported particularly in societies where women have to bear the dual burden of earner and home nurturer and carer. Stress may be caused by situational factors, such as occupational patterns and organization of work; high pollution levels and changes in climate—particularly the rising of temperature in tropical countries, along with narrowing of diurnal temperature *range* witnessed in cities like Kolkata—may be other important factors.

6.3 Globalization and Risk

The crux of our argument is that globalization affects sexual behaviour primarily in two ways. On the one hand, as we have seen, the social disruption and cultural change relax norms inhibiting sexuality as the local attitude towards sexuality is replaced by more permissive global norms and attitudes.[1] On the other hand, we argue, the economic foundations on which the globalized society is built upon expose the individual to more risk and stress. While preindustrial societies were also characterized by risk, globalization has changed the nature and quantum of risk. In this section, we examine the notion of risk in society and its implications.

6.3.1 Risk and "Risk Society"

The term "risk society" is associated with the names of Antony Giddens (1990, 1991) and Ulrich Beck (1992). Before the era of modernity, risk was a neutral term, concerned merely with probabilities, with losses and gains. A gamble or an

[1]The result is not a unilinear movement towards a more permissive society. Clashes can, and do, occur between traditional structures and agents of change. This may lead to temporary rollbacks.

endeavour that was associated with high risk meant simply that there was great potential for significant loss or significant reward. This is reflected in economist's theories about profit as a reward for bearing risk and uncertainty (Knight 1921). However, in the modern period, risk has been co-opted as a term reserved for a negative or undesirable outcome, so that it has become synonymous with the terms danger or hazard. For instance, the British Medical Association's (1987: 13) guide *Living with Risk* describes a hazard as "a set of circumstances which may cause harmful consequences", while risk is "the likelihood of its doing so" (cited in Fox 1999: 12).

In Western cultures, the latter half of the twentieth century has been described as an epoch of flux, uncertainty, and rapid social change (Bauman 1991; Marwick 1990). During this period, distinct transformations in the structure and functions of dominant institutions generated a complex mix of liberties and constraints (Giddens 1991, Waters 1995). Since the Second World War, the building blocks of society have effectively been shaken up and relaid. Far-reaching transformations in family structure, employment patterns, and welfare provision have redrawn class boundaries, shuffled gender roles, and chopped up social identities (Beck 2000; Hughes and Fergusson 2000). As Beck points out, modernization is associated with:

> ... surges of technological rationalization and changes in work and organization, but beyond that includes much more: the change in societal characteristics and normal biographies, changes in lifestyle and forms of love, change in the structures of power and influence, in the forms of political repression and participation, in views of reality and in the norms of knowledge. In social science's understanding of modernity, the plough, the steam locomotive and the microchip are visible indicators of a much deeper process, which comprises and reshapes the entire social structure (Beck 1992: 50).

As the twenty-first century unfolds, the process of globalization continues to disperse through economies and political institutions, rendering visible the connections between global shifts and local actions (Robertson 1992; Tomlinson 1999). Economic convergence, political fluctuation, and national insecurity have become the motifs of the age. We are living in a "runaway world" stippled by ominous dangers, military conflicts, and environmental hazards. Moreover, the hazards are taking an increasingly visible form. As a result, increasing portions of our everyday lives are spent negotiating change, dealing with uncertainty, and assessing the personal impacts of situations that appear to be out of our control. In one way or another, the defining markers of modern society are all associated with the phenomenon of risk. In contemporary culture, risk has become something of an omnipresent issue, casting its spectre over a wide range of practices and experiences (Adam and van Loon 2000: 2; Lupton 1999: 14). Locally, risk emerges as a routine feature of existence in areas as diverse as health, parenting, crime, employment and transport. (Mythen 2004: 1).

Beck argues that the risk inherent in modern society contributes in the above ways towards the formation of a global *risk society*. The technological change forming the crux of modernization produces new forms of risks to which society has to constantly respond and adjust. While Beck's focus is on environmental and health risks, it also includes a whole series of interrelated changes within contemporary social life such as shifting employment patterns, heightened job insecurity, declining influence of tradition and custom, erosion of traditional family patterns, and democratization of personal relations.

What is important about these risks is that they are not restricted to one country only. As countries become more interconnected with the implanting of Western institutions and work and lifestyles in developing countries, the risks spill over to affect all countries and all social classes.

6.3.2 New Forms of Risk in Modern Society

In a special lecture in the Third Asian Population Conference, Gietel-Basten (2015) had argued that living in a risk society can have profound implications for sexual and reproductive practices. The implication of risk society for sexuality, however, is an issue that has remained unexplored so far.

We argue that technology and globalization have changed not only the quantum of risk but its form and how it is manifested. For instance, in preindustrial society with underdeveloped health facilities, risk was cantered upon mortality and survival. A crucial problem in such societies was the high infant and maternal mortality rates. The insurance was, as demographers have pointed out, high fertility rates—assuming that with a large family would ensure that at least one son survives to take care of the parents. As health facilities have developed and lowered infant and maternal death rates, removing this risk, societies enter into the third stage of demographic transition with falling fertility rates. While the theory states that the desire for increasing standard of living will spur the demand for restricting family size, a more nuanced explanation can be sought by exploring the conflicts, tensions, and challenges of a risk society. In particular, we have to examine the conflict produced by changes in the labour market. Integration of domestic markets with global markets, along with the need to cater to foreign customers, has resulted in the introduction of new work patterns and employment strategies copied from the West. This, along with the increasing entry of women into high-paying and technical jobs, creates new forms of risks and tensions.

Friedman (2000) argued that if the defining anxiety of the Cold War was fear of nuclear annihilation, the defining anxiety of globalization is fear of rapid change—"a sense that your job, community or workplace can be changed at any moment by anonymous economic and technological forces that are anything but stable" (Friedman 2000: 12). This fear may lead workers to work harder and over longer hours, resulting in physical and mental stress. The change in organization of work may also contribute to increasing stress in many ways. "Modern working life also changes constantly due to rapid scientific and technological advances. Consequently, rapid changes in production systems take place" (Houtman and Jettinghoff 2007: 8). This means that workers have to deal with stress caused by:

(a) increased demands of learning new skills,
(b) the need to adopt new ways of working,
(c) the pressure of the demand for higher productivity,
(d) demands for increased quality of work,
(e) increased time pressure and hectic jobs,
(f) higher job competition,
(g) increased job insecurity and less benefits, and
(h) less time for co-workers and socializing.

While research on the relationship between globalization, work, and stress is a recently emerging area, there is already sufficient evidence to suggest that globalization leads to physical and mental stress and fatigue.

In many sectors, where workers are part of a team, stress and impaired performance may spill over to other workers in the team (Chopra 2009). Co-workers may need to perform additional work to compensate (Dewa et al. 2007). Stress may also "spill over" effects to the individual's family members, who may themselves be employed or engaged in other social responsibilities (Chopra 2009).

Houtman and Jettinghoff (2007) have pointed out that "Work related stress in developing countries is often made worse by broad spectrum of factors outside the work environment" (Houtman and Jettinghoff 2007: 6). These factors include poor environmental management of pollution, inadequate transportation system, and gender inequalities. Pollution may affect physical health, causing fatigue and sapping the vitality of the worker. This may be reinforced by the poor transportation system characterizing cities of many developing countries. Travelling to the working place, or returning from work, in hot and humid conditions in overcrowded public transports that are neither regular nor very frequent tires out an already tired out worker. Climate change leading to a rise in the daily average or maximum temperature is important. But more important is the change in minimum temperature. This also rises, and if it rises at a faster rate than maximum temperature then it leads to a narrowing down of the range of temperature, preventing the cooling off of the body at night.

Social organization producing gender inequalities may also increase stress in many ways. In the working place, women workers have reported the pressure of being a minority group, generally excluded from peer group social interaction.

Work-related stress may additionally result from a poor balance at the home-work interface….. This would particularly affect women in countries where gender disparities are strong and women have had a recent involvement in the workforce. Responsibilities at work may conflict with family responsibilities such as care for a sick child or an elderly relative, or commitments to family and friends. Spillover effects between work and home responsibilities showed to be one of the best predictors of psychological strain among women workers across hierarchical levels and sectors (Cedillo and Scarone 2005, in Houtman and Jettinghoff 2007: 18).

In a study of women workers in Kolkata's IT sector, respondents reported the psychological burden of being expected to undertake household and childcare related activities in addition to completing office assignments (Husain and Dutta 2013). While such women often employed maid servants and cooks as substitutes, they reported the constant fear that such persons would be absent. Respondents also reported that male colleagues are generally insensitive to child-related problems:

> "There are people … when you call up to say that you will be working from home because your maid hasn't turned up and you have to look after your daughter … people don't say it but you feel it that men don't think … realise that this is an issue—but it matters a lot to you.… No one will say it why you are doing this…because that is going against the code of conduct and also that would take away the liberated image from them" (cited in Husain and Dutta 2013: 156).

An ITES employee said that when she left early, her colleagues perceived her to be slacking. This also creates tension and stress.

Similar experiences are reported in other Asian countries. Gietel-Basten (2015) quotes a Chinese respondent declaiming:

"I don't want to have other children. My partner has little time to take care of our child. Before our first child went to kindergarten, it was almost just me taking care of him. It was really tiring…. So we don't have the condition to have other children. My husband hardly devoted any energy when we had our first child, and he never changed a nappy for our baby… he basically did not take care of the child in the evening. The idea to have another kid drives me crazy! I think I cannot handle that."

Another respondent from Taipei comments:

"I think a lot of people would choose that one child is the best if they decide to have children. It really impacts the decision whether they would like to have more children or not. If they have more children, can they really afford it? Whether my job can survive or not when my family has more children? Whether my busy working hours can support more children or not? This has definitely its impact".

In other words, as societies in developing countries have modernized, the pre-modern risks and conflicts governing fertility decisions have changed. Greater integration with Western societies has led to the reorganization of urban production systems imposing new demands upon the labour force. The increasing female work-force participation (particularly their entry into blue and pink collar jobs), coupled with recognition of their rights (including those in the sexual domain), increasing aspirations and control over fertility decisions creates new forms of tensions that influence decisions regarding whether to marry, when to marry, whether to have children, and how many. Consequently, fertility control and planning become a conscious decision:

> "… the greater the attendant risks, uncertainties and demands, the more does having children cease to be a natural part of life, and become the object of conscious planning and calculation, hopes and fears" (Beck and Beck-Gernsheim 2002: 126).

Simultaneously, quantity of children no longer remains the central concern of family planning in risk societies. Given that technological advances have ensured that the child will survive, the focus is now on quality. The objective of parents is to invest in their children in such a manner that they have a bright future. This calls for a decline in fertility and associated change in fertility plans—the third stage in demographic transition. Consequently, sexuality looses its value as a means of procreation and becomes more a means of pleasure. “Modern” perceptions about sexuality and accepted sexual behaviour imported from the West, via the Internet and other forms of mass media and communication, are factors that facilitate this transition.

6.3.3 Stress, Sexuality, and Fertility in a Risk Society

The consensus among researchers on workplace dynamics and stress is that, while globalization may have encouraged a more sexually permissive society, it has also led to an increase in physical and mental stress and fatigue—factors that may adversely affect sexuality. While the impact of these factors on sexuality has to be explored, there is enough evidence to hypothesize a plausible relationship between the globalization, workplace dynamics, stress, and sexuality.

In the previous section, we have seen how organization of work produces stress. This affects sexuality. For instance, certain sectors, such as the IT and ITES sectors, are associated with long hours of work. Apart from the long hours, the work timings may often be uncertain. When the wife also works in a similar job, matching of shifts may not occur. Further, a partner may be absent for a long time on offshore assignments. While such problems are important when *both* partners work in the IT and ITES sector, the engagement of even the wife in such occupations may affect marital relations. In one case, the male respondent reported to have refused to marry a girl working in the back office of a MNC bank because she worked in night shifts. He justified his refusal by the statement: “When she comes in I will be going out for work”.

Even in daily life, factors such as work-related pressure, poor and overcrowded transport, requirement of household chores, and need to supervise education of child produce stress. While some factors affect both partners, the women are generally more affected as they have to bear the dual burden of work and home care.

Space and privacy are also important. Bancroft points out that “Overcrowding and unsuitable circumstances frequently spoil intimacy or even prevent it from becoming established” (1993: 104). In the case of poor households, for instance, sexuality is a normal part of everyday life:

> “Let us look into the poverty stricken home of the proletariat! In narrow, unclean apartment the lives of adults in the family and also foreign bed-renters plays out shamelessly in front of the eyes of children of all ages. Filthy discussions, tendernesses, sexual acts, births—all are openly paraded in front of the children of all ages; children sleep with their parents, one or more siblings, even those of the opposite sex share the same bed, ...” (Friedjung 1926: 1)

In the case of educated middle-class families—where overt display of sexuality is prohibited by social norms—the search for private space has given rise to nuclear families. Although this may have solved the privacy issue to some extent, the solution has a cost. The absence of older generations within the household implies that the responsibility for undertaking household tasks and looking after the child falls entirely upon the parents, particularly women.[2]

> "Women are increasingly caught in a dilemma, since there are inadequate facilities for them to combine job and family, and they get only limited help from men with children. The outcome is a historically new constellation, in which many women have a strong desire for children but, if they act on this wish, have to reckon with considerable costs for their own life in terms of limited job opportunities, excessive daily workloads, reduced leisure, financial insecurity on old age, and a risk of poverty in the event of divorce" (Beck-Gernsheim 2007: 72, cited in Gietel-Basten 2015).

Consequently, most families are being increasingly motivated to regulate fertility and restrict the number of children to generally one, at most two. This leads to concentration of investment, in contrast to the earlier strategy of risk diversification.

6.3.4 Generation Me and Sexuality

The findings of a recent US government on sexuality are relevant and provide some evidence in support of our hypothesis (Martinez and Abma 2015). The report observes that the new generation who had attained adulthood in 2000, referred to as Millennials or Generation Me (because of their narcissm), is the first generation who have less sex than their parents did at the same age. This is in line with another study conducted by Dr. Jean Twenge of San Diego University, who reported that millennials were not only likely to have less sex but also likely to have a lower number of sexual partners (Twenge 2014). The average number of partners, which peaked in the 1960s, has fallen from 4 to 3.5 in the 1980s generation. What is surprising is that this trend is occurring despite the reportedly more permissive attitude of the millennials towards sex (Twenge et al. 2015) (Fig. 6.2).

The shift in sexual behaviour is the result of a unique mix of socio-economic circumstances. The millennials are saddled with student debt and entered the labour market at a time when the world economy entered a recessionary phase. As a result they work for longer hours, generally in insecure jobs. Privacy is a major issue for this generation as rising rentals force them to share flats with family members or non-relatives. As Twinge points out:

> "When you're a young adult living with your parents, it's harder to have sex. Even though the recession is over, more young adults are still living with their parents. It's like being a young teen again, trying to figure out where to get some privacy. Having flatmates can make this difficult too—you're afraid they will hear your activities, and they might not

[2]This has lead to the phenomenon of "living together but separately", with the maintaining of multigenerational ties even though they do not reside together. This is particularly important in the case of child care (Husain and Dutta 2013).

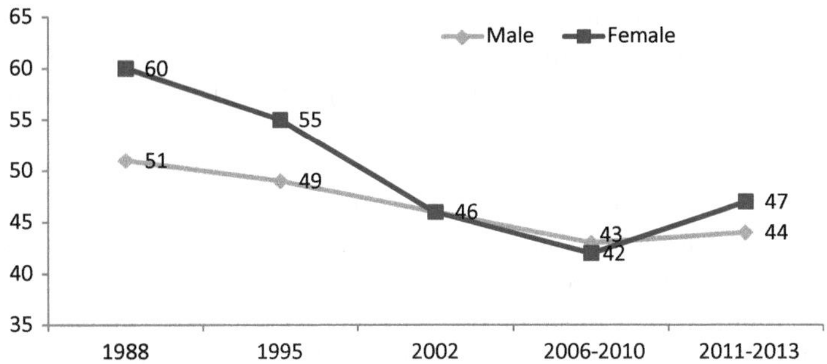

Fig. 6.2 Never-married females and males aged 15–19 who have ever had sexual intercourse: United States, 1988–2013. *Source* Adapted from Martinez and Abma (2015)

> appreciate having someone else in their space. It's also more difficult because fewer young men have jobs, and most young women want to date someone who is employed" (Twinge, cited in Fenton 2016).

Another important factor is the Internet. The millennials have greater access to and use the Internet more intensively. This causes a digital overload as easy access to pornographic material has been reported to have youths away from sexual intercourse, with digital pornography becoming a substitute for physical relations with a real person.

6.4 Some Qualitative Information

The impact of such a risk society on sexuality is a topic that has not been explored by Indian researchers. It is quite likely that risk and stress will affect the incidence of intercourse, fertility plans, and contraception choice. The increasing incidence of premarital sex, delayed marriage, and women who choose not to marry in Indian society reflects how society adjusts to these new challenges. After marriage, delayed or not, the decision to limit number of children and their timings is a form of this adjustment.[3] This section provides some ethnographic evidence from our survey in support of this theory.

As mentioned before, about five percent of our sample was interviewed in some more details. No questionnaire was used—field investigators asked respondents about the frequency of cohabitation and contraceptive choice. We did not explore the work-home conflict and the stress of work as these are issues that have been explored in enough details in other studies; further, they do not comprise the central focus of our study. Rather, we sought to examine how living in a risk society

[3]An interesting strategy to minimize such conflict is to adopt children straightaway, without trying to have children of their own.

impacts sexuality, fertility planning, and choice of contraception method. Given the confidential nature of these issues, responses were predictably not forthcoming and were mostly evasive in nature. The ethnographic evidence that we did get is summarized below.

In the immediate postmarriage phase, when sexual activity is at its peak, the need for means to regulate fertility is also correspondingly high. This stage is also marked by lack of awareness about the reproductive processes and contraception methods, coupled with inexperience. This calls for reliance on an "infallible" and easy to use contraception method. Respondents reported the perception that condoms generally satisfy this need. Although pills can fulfil this need, the fear of side effects restricts reliance on pills.

As the marriage matures, reproduction becomes a dominant motive underlying sexual intercourse. The need to control fertility looses importance temporarily. Couples either stop using any contraception methods or shift to behavioural methods.

After the first conception, the frequency of sexual intercourse declines over time.

> "Married or not, people have significantly less sex as they get older, although decline in the frequency of sex has more to do with the length of marriage or the relationship than with age. The frequency of sex varies according to culture. Sex after the age of 40 is significantly lower in some parts of Asia compared with the West. In India, for example, many couples abstain from sex at 50, or where a woman has a married daughter or becomes a grandmother" (MacKay 2001: 74).

This may also be attributed to the pressures of living in a risk society. Working respondents reported that they were so tired after completing household chores and their children that they preferred intercourse during weekends or during holidays and wanted a method that could be used without any preparation. Non-working respondents, on the other hand, reported a greater degree of flexibility. As they do not have to bear the dual burden of work and home responsibilities, they are less exhausted and reportedly allow their husband greater flexibility in time of intercourse and contraception method.

Simultaneously, families also consciously decide not to have any children. This is dictated not by desire to maintain standard of living (as suggested by the demographic theory of transition), but the high opportunity cost of having a child in risk societies—resulting in a decision to curtail number of children. When respondents were asked about the ideal family size, most opted for a four-member family. The reason underlying the perception of two children being ideal was the perception that a single child would not have enough company and may become a loner, developing psychological problems. We did not find any son preference in choice of children. Generally, respondents reported that they wanted to have one son and one daughter. In that case, if a couple already has a daughter (son) they want a son (daughter).

Subsequently, however, the pressure of looking after one child generally becomes too much, so that families abandon the desire to have the second child. Respondents have expressed their feelings about stress and work pressure, at home and in the office, very strongly and underlined that this is a major factor determining actual family size. Therefore, we can see, after the first child is born, there is a decline in the incidence of sexual activity coupled by a strong desire to limit fertility.

The demand to restrict fertility is facilitated by coming into contact with gynaecologists, during pregnancy and subsequently, who can provide necessary knowledge about contraception methods. However, once again, the pressures of residing in the risk society remain a dominant factor determining choice of contraception method.

Respondents had reported that work patterns dictate the frequency and timings of sexual intercourse. Another important factor dictating the frequency of sexual intercourse is the sleeping habit. There is a very important difference in sleeping patterns between Indian and Western couples—in India (and in many Asian countries), the child normally sleeps with parents in their bed till seven–eight years or till another child is born. This restricts sexual activity to occasions when the child visits his/her grandparents or other relatives, or when the child sleeps with visiting relatives. In such cases, given that the opportunity for cohabitation becomes a matter of chance, the contraception method has to be chosen so that it may be adopted without prior preparation and easily used/discarded.

Permanent methods such as IUD or Copper T, or contraceptive pills, are not very suitable as they have to be continued with as long as there is the probability of sexual activity in the immediate future—however, low the likelihood. Condoms may be purchased and stored for use. But, given the lack of private space in Indian middle-class families, storage over a long period risks discovery by elderly relatives or even children—offending cultural norms. Mukherjee (2009) cites a husband stating "… we used this method because we felt this is the easiest method. After marriage I used condom, but there are several problems viz. buying, disposing; and we had started using this withdrawal method". Further, respondents reported that husbands were generally "lazy" and reluctant to adopt condoms—they preferred the contraceptive to be adopted by their wives. The fear of losing their erection (reported in Rogow and Horowitz 1995) and reluctance to purchase it from distributors (reported in Frick-Bruder 1980) also contributes to this "laziness". This was also confirmed by the ethnographic evidence from our study. In such circumstances, methods such as withdrawal and rhythm, in isolation or in combination, provide a compromise solution suiting male preference and the comfort of the wife.

6.5 Summing up

Our analysis finds a high extent of reliance on behavioural methods among urban educated women in West Bengal. This is observed in both data from NFHS and also from the primary survey. Attempts to explain this phenomenon using either the ultra-modern contraception hypothesis or son preference fails. In fact, both approaches have certain limitations. Attempts at addressing these inadequacies lead us to study *combinations* of contraception methods and, more important, how the choice of means to control fertility varies over the reproductive life cycle. Such analysis reveals that the reliance on behavioural methods is not constant over the life cycle but displays a U-shaped trend. Moreover, the choice seems to be dictated by attempts to adjust to a globalized sex characterized by physical and mental stress, uncertainty, lack of space and privacy, along with greater permissiveness and sexual awareness. The conflict between remnants of the old society (more relaxed but also prohibitive) and the emerging globalized risk society (permissive but hectic) shapes the environment in the bedroom and influences both sexuality and the means to regulate fertility. Given the irregular nature of intercourse, the search for contraception methods which can be easily used and discarded leads to a reliance on behavioural methods.

References

Adam, B., & van Loon, J. (2000). Repositioning risk: The challenge for social theory. In B. Adam, U. Beck, & J. van Loon (Eds.), *The risk society and beyond*. London: Sage.

Altman, D. (2001). *Global sex*. Chicago: University of Chicago Press.

Altman, D. (2004). Sexuality and globalization. *Sexuality Research & Social Policy, 1*(1), 63–68.

Bancroft, J. (1993). Impact of environment, stress, occupational, and other hazards on sexuality and sexual behavior. *Environmental Health Perspectives Supplements, 101*(Suppl. 2), 101–107.

Bauman, Z. (1991). *Modernity and ambivalence*. Cambridge: Polity Press.

Beck, U. (1992). *Risk society: Towards a new modernity*. London: Sage.

Beck, U. (2000). *Brave new world of work*. Cambridge: Polity Press.

Beck, U., & Beck-Gernsheim, E. (2002). *Individualization: Institutionalized individualism and its social and political consequences*. London: Sage.

Billy, J. O. G., Brewster, K. L., & Grady, W. R. (1994). Contextual effects on the sexual behavior of adolescent women. *Journal of Marriage and Family, 56*(2), 387–404.

Brewster, K. L. (1994). Neighborhood context and the transition to sexual activity among young black women. *Demography, 31*(4), 603–614.

Brewster, K. L., Billy, J. O. G., & Grady, W. R. (1993). Social context and adolescent behavior: The impact of community on the transition to sexual activity. *Social Forces, 71*(3), 713–740.

British Medical Association. (1987). *Living with risk*. Chichester: WIley.

Browning, C. R., & Olinger-Wilbon, M. (2003). Neighborhood structure, social organization, and number of short-term sexual partnerships. *Journal of Marriage and Family, 65*(3), 730–745.

Cedillo, B. L., & Scarone, M. (2005). Psychosocial risk factors for women workers and psychological strain. Oral presentation. Abstract F4-1. Book of Abstracts. 2nd ICOH International Conference on Psychosocial Factors at Work. Okayama, Japan. August.

Chopra, P. (2009). Mental health and the workplace: Issues for developing countries. *International Journal of Mental Health Systems, 3*(4). www.ijhms.com/content/3/I/4. Accessed May 12, 2016.

Crosby, R., Holtgrave, D., DiClemente, R. J., Wingood, G., & Gayle, J. (2003). Social capital as a predictor of adolescents' sexual risk behavior: A state-level exploratory study. *AIDS and Behavior, 7*(3), 245–252.

Dewa, C. S., McDaid, D., & Ettner, S. L. (2007). An international perspective on worker mental health problems: who bears the burden and how are costs addressed. *Canadian Journal of Psychiatry, 52*(6), 346–356.

Fenton, S. (2016). Why millennials stopped having sex. Independent 7 July 2016. http://ind.pn/29qdu5f. Accessed July 8, 2016.

Fox, N. J. (1999). Postmodern reflections on 'risks', 'hazards' and life choices. In D. Lupton (Ed.), *Risk and socio-cultural theory: New directions and perspectives*. Cambridge: Cambridge University Press.

Frick-Bruder, V. (1980). Kontrazeptionsmethoden und Sexuelles Empfiden. *Zeitschrift fur Allgemeinmedizin, 56*(1), 47–49.

Friedjung, J. (1926). *Die Geschlechliche Aufklärung in Erziehungswerke: Ein Wegweiser fur Eltern*. Erzieher und Ărzte: Verlag von Josef Safár, Wien.

Friedman, T. L. (2000). *The Lexus and the olive tree*. New York: Anchor Books.

Frye, V., Latka, M. H., Koblin, B., Halkitis, P., Putnam, S., Galea, S., et al. (2006). The urban environment and sexual risk behavior among men who have sex with men. *Journal of Urban Health, 83*(2), 308–324.

Giddens, A. (1990). *Consequences of modernity*. Cambridge: Polity Press.

Giddens, A. (1991). *Modernity and self-identity. Self and society in the late modern age*. Stanford: Stanford University Press.

Gietel-Basten, S. (2015). Individualisation, risk society and ultra-low fertility. Plenary lecture delivered at third asian population conference, Kuala Lumpur, 26–30 July.

Houtman, I., & Jettinghoff, K. (2007). Raising awareness of stress at work in developing countries. Protecting Workers Health Series No. 6. Geneva, World Health Organization.

Hughes, G., & Fergusson, R. (2000). *Ordering lives: Family. Work and welfare*. London: Routledge.

Husain, Z., & Dutta, M. (2013). *Women in Kolkata's IT sector: Satisficing between work and household*. New Delhi: Springer.

Knight, F. (1921). *Risk, uncertainty and profit*. Boston, MA: Hart, Schaffner & Marx.

Lupton, D. (1999). *Risk*. London: Routledge.

Mackay, J. (2001). Global sex: Sexuality and sexual practices around the world. *Sexual and Relationship Therapy, 16*(1), 71–82.

Martinez, G. M., & Abma, J. C. (2015). Sexual activity, contraceptive use, and childbearing of teenagers aged 15–19 in the United States. NCHS Data Brief No. 209. Atlanta: National Centre for Health Statistics. http://www.cdc.gov/nchs/data/databriefs/db209.pdf. Accessed July 8, 2015.

Marwick, A. (1990). *British Society since 1945*. London: Penguin.

Mukherjee, S. (2009). Abortion as a process of birth limiting rather spacing among the traditional method of contraceptive users in West Bengal. *Paper presented in 26th International seminar of International Union for Scientific Studies in Population, Marrakech, Morocco, 27 September–2 October*.

Mythen, G. (2004). *Ulrich Beck: A critical introduction to the risk society*. London: Pluto Press.

Ramirez-Valles, J., Zimmerman, M. A., & Newcomb, M. D. (1998). Sexual risk behavior among youth: Modeling the influence of prosocial activities and socioeconomic factors. *Journal of Health and Social Behavior, 39*(3), 237–253.

Robertson, R. (1992). *Globalization: Social theory and global culture*. London: Sage.

Rogow, D., & Horowitz, S. (1995). Withdrawal: A review of the literature and an agenda for research. *Studies in Family Planning, 26*, 140–153.

South, S. J., & Lloyd, K. F. (1995). Spousal alternatives and marital dissolution. *American Social Review, 60*(1), 21–35.

Stack, S. (1994). Relocation: the effect of geographic mobility on premarital sex. *Journal of Marriage and Family, 56*(1), 204–208.

Tomlinson, J. (1999). *Globalization and culture*. Cambridge: Polity Press.

Turner, B. S. (2010). Theories of globalization: Issues and origins. In: Turner BS (ed.), *The Routledge international handbook of globalization studies*. Routledge: Oxon.

Twenge, J. M., Sherman, R. A., & Wells, B. E. (2015). Changes in American Adults' sexual behavior and attitudes, 1972–2012. *Archive of Sexual Behaviour, 44*(8), 2273–2285.

Twenge, J. M. (2014). Generation Me. Revised and Updated version. Atria Press, London.

Upchurch, D. M., Aneshensel, C. S., Sucoff, C. A., & Levy-Storms, L. (1999). Neighborhood and family contexts of adolescent sexual activity. *Journal of Marriage and Family, 61*(4), 920–933.

Waters, M. (1995). *Key ideas: Globalization*. London: Routledge.

Chapter 7
Behavioural Contraception Methods and Urban Graduates: Summing Up the Evidence

Abstract This chapter sums up our findings with respect to the following questions:

- What is the proportion of women relying on behavioural contraceptive methods in India? Has it changed over time?
- What is the socio-economic profile of users of behavioural methods in India? Is it true that it is the urban elite who rely on this method?
- Is use of such methods higher in certain regions, particularly in the state West Bengal?
- How reliable is this method in terms of controlling fertility?
- What explains the reliance on behavioural methods?
- Do couples rely solely on this method? Or do they combine methods? Further, does the method mix vary over the reproductive life cycle of women?

Finally, our study also questions the mainstream approach to contraception choice. In large-scale surveys on reproductive health, the focus is on current and ever use of contraception, with the implicit assumption that the respondent uses a single method at a point of time. Actual contraception choice is more complex. Women may use not a single method, but combination of methods. Even this combination may change over time. Further, the choice of method or their combinations is determined by factors determining frequency and timing of intercourse, such as the stress of living in a globalized risk society, occupation, working habits, and sleeping patterns. We argue that incorporating these issues in large-scale surveys on reproductive health is a major challenge that policy makers and researchers must face in the coming decades.

Keywords Behavioural methods · Contraception choice · Risk society · Urban elite

Z. Husain and M. Dutta, *Fertility Control in a Risk Society*,
SpringerBriefs in Population Studies, DOI 10.1007/978-81-322-3685-6_7

7.1 Returning to Research Questions

Modern contraceptives have been promoted by policy makers in developing countries with a view to reduce fertility and control spread of RTI/STI. Aggressive campaigning by pharmaceutical companies and the popular media, leading to the "medicalization" of the female body in recent years (Thapan 1997, 2009; Uberoi and Bahadur 2001), also seeks to create a demand for modern contraception products, like contraception pills. However, some of these products have side effects and inconvenience users (Jejeebhoy and Xavier 2012; Rajaretnam and Deshpande 1994; Sedgh et al. 2007). Further, methods like IUD require the assistance of paramedical/medical personnel, reducing their popularity. Specific methods have often aroused controversy due to their adverse side effects and forcible nature of implementation.[1]

In this context, behavioural contraception methods are believed to offer a choice of methods that are reliable, do not have any adverse medical side effects, and may be conveniently used by the couple possessing necessary skill/knowledge. Thus, they appear to be superior to modern contraceptives. This study examines the use of behavioural methods among currently married educated women in India, focusing on the metropolitan city of Kolkata, the motives underlying choice of such methods and the relationship between reliance on behavioural methods and fertility. In particular, we seek answers to the following research questions:

- What is the proportion of women relying on behavioural contraceptive methods in India? Has it changed over time?
- What is the socio-economic profile of users of behavioural methods in India? Is it true that it is the urban elite who rely on this method?
- Is use of such methods higher in certain regions, particularly in the state West Bengal?
- How reliable is this method in terms of controlling fertility?
- What explains the reliance on behavioural methods?
- Do couples rely solely on this method? Or do they combine methods? Further, does the method mix vary over the reproductive life cycle of women?

The answers to these issues, as revealed in our analysis, are summarized below.

7.1.1 How Popular Are Behavioural Methods?

As shown in Chap. 2, the literature on family planning methods has tended to view behavioural methods as an archaic method, ineffective in controlling fertility, and

[1]Such controversies arose in India over forced vasectomy during the emergency, introduction of Norplant-R in the 1990s, etc. The recent anecdotal evidence that sterilization is occurring without informed consent of women may also be mentioned.

the resort of women who are either uneducated or lack access to educational facilities or belong to specific religious groups (Roman Catholics and Muslims). The Indian literature, too, is no exception.

Analysis of the data for all the three rounds of National Family Health Survey (NFHS) reveals, however, that both withdrawal and rhythm are used, if not widely, at least by a substantial proportion of currently married women in India. Further, the incidence of use of behavioural methods has not fallen, but has increased marginally at the all-India level. Considerable regional variations may also be observed, with the use of behavioural methods being higher in East Indian states such as West Bengal, Assam, and Tripura. The use of behavioural methods is also found to be higher among the Bengali-speaking community, irrespective of their location.

Further, the use of behavioural methods is not restricted to women residing in rural areas, from low-income families and lacking education, nor it is restricted to women who may lack access to family planning facilities. In fact, such women are specifically targeted by government family planning methods and tend to rely on modern methods, particularly sterilization. This is not surprising, but simply an example of supply induced demand. Who, then, are the users of behavioural methods?

Basu (2005) had argued, in line with studies of behavioural methods in other countries, that it was currently married women at the other end of the socio-economic stratum who were the main users of behavioural methods. Her conclusions, however, were based on the first round of NFHS only. Our analysis of NFHS data reveals that her conclusions hold for the other two rounds also—women who have at least twelve years of education, reside in urban areas, and belong to the top 40 % of the Standard of Living Index (SLI) quintile are the main users of such methods. They are referred to as the urban elite by Basu (2005). When we narrow our focus to the state of West Bengal, analysis of NFHS data again shows that it is this socio-economic class who are the main users of behavioural methods.

This claim is also vindicated by the primary survey of currently married graduate women undertaken in Kolkata, the capital of West Bengal and a major metropolitan city in India. Reliance on behavioural methods, particularly withdrawal, is found to be high. About two-thirds of respondents reported ever use of behavioural methods. Withdrawal is the most popular method, followed by male condoms; rhythm appears a third choice among users. In particular, use of behavioural methods is high among the Bengali community, residents in North Kolkata and Salt Lake and those with relatively low Standard of Living Index (SLI) scores. Although religion is expected to play an important role, we did not find a higher incidence of reliance on behavioural methods among Muslims and Christians. This may be attributed to the nature of our sample—urban, educated, and well-off. Such households do recognize the need for family planning. Among Muslims, modern and more liberal interpretations of the *Shariat* too have helped to increase the adoption of contraception methods.[2] Caste, too, does not have any impact on contraception choice.

The urban elite are likely to have well-defined fertility plans, with fertility levels equal to or below replacement level; they also have access to birth control measures. Why such women use supposedly outdated and ineffective methods is worth examining? Two issues are important here: Are behavioural methods really ineffective? What are the factors that lead the urban elite to rely on such methods?

7.1.2 Behavioural Methods and Fertility Control

There is some controversy over whether behavioural methods are really able to control fertility effectively. The scientific evidence is that withdrawal is about as effective as male condoms in preventing pregnancy. To what extent rhythm and withdrawal are actually able to control parity depends upon the skill and knowledge of users.

Both literature (Juarez et al. 2009; Gray et al. 1997) and our own analysis of NFHS data indicate that even the urban elite, in developing countries, may often lack the skill and knowledge to practice traditional methods effectively. We have shown that a substantial proportion of women practising behavioural methods are unable to identify their safe periods correctly. But this finding should be treated with caution as the spread of Western attitudes and culture through the media in recent years have removed the social restrictions and shame associated with discussing sexual practices and family planning methods within and outside the family. Access to medical practitioners and Internet, coupled with more openness in discussing family planning methods among family members and friends, has reduced the ignorance about ovulatory periods. It is not surprising that our survey contradicts the NFHS results to show that the majority of women are aware about safe periods and are theoretically capable of using the rhythm method capably.

In this context, the method of assessing success in controlling fertility is also important. Basu (2005) and Johnson-Hanks (2002) have suggested that number of live births should be used to assess the effectiveness of behavioural methods to regulate fertility. On the basis of number of live births, they have shown that behavioural methods are successfully used by the urban elite to regulate fertility. In Italy, similarly, couples were reportedly masters and mistresses of their own fertility in the early part of the twentieth century (Schneider and Schneider 1996). While this is supported by our findings—based on analysis of both NFHS and primary data—the number of *conceptions* may be a more accurate means of evaluating the

[2]This finding questions the half-baked theories propounded by Sharma and Pasha (2011) and provides support to Iyer's hypothesis that it is economic status and lack of access that are the main causes of low contraceptive prevalence rate among Muslims (Iyer 2002).

effectiveness of behavioural methods to control fertility. In Italy, after the 1970s, use of behavioural methods has been associated with a high rate of unintended pregnancies (Gribaldo et al. 2009). A similar finding is reported by studies of behavioural method use in other Afro-Asian countries (Castiglioni et al. 2001; Dalla Zuanna et al. 2005; Erfani and Yuksel-Kaptanoglu 2012; Johnson-Hanks 2002; Kovavisarach and Saringcarnan 2010; Nguyen and Miller 2012). While data on the number of conceptions is not collected in NFHS, the incidence of medically terminated pregnancies (MTPs) provides an estimate of the number of conceptions—given that the number of live children does not vary significantly between users of modern and behavioural contraception methods. The incidence of unplanned pregnancies (collected in the primary survey) is also an indication. The evidence from both NFHS and the primary survey shows that use of behavioural methods may be associated with high failure rates.

Despite reliance on behavioural methods, respondents of our survey perceived such methods, particularly withdrawal, to be unreliable. About 27 % of women whose husbands used withdrawal reported that their husbands had failed to withdraw in time. Although women were aware of their "safe" periods, the changes in the monthly cycle with age often created problems. About 37 % of rhythm users reported a failure to calculate the safe period. It was not surprising, therefore, that the incidence of unintended pregnancy was high—17 % and 21 % for withdrawal and rhythm, respectively. The failure rate among users of withdrawal and rhythm was estimated to be 23 and 16 %, respectively.

7.1.3 Cultural Dissent, or Son Preference?

We next examine possible motives underlying choice of contraception method. The main motives are ease of use and preference of husband. The latter is interesting as it conflicts with the claim made by the majority of respondents that contraception choice is a joint decision. Reliability and (physical) comfort (of the user) are relatively less important methods. We also found that users were reluctant to use contraceptive pills over a long period because of real or imagined side effects. While this may appear to reflect the natural–technological dichotomy referred to in literature (Basu 2005; Johnson-Hanks 2002), one should be cautious in accepting this interpretation.

Given the higher number of *conceptions* but same number of *births* among users of behavioural methods vis-à-vis users of modern methods, it is obvious that fertility control is attained by the former through emergency contraception or induced abortion—both of which are detrimental for reproductive health, fecundity, and mental health of the women. Our survey found that in over 90 % of such unintended pregnancies, respondents reported having taken recourse to techno-medical means to terminate the pregnancy, with emergency contraceptive pills being a common recourse for 53 % of women reporting method failure.

In addition, if the woman has more than one sexual partner—a phenomenon which has been observed to increase sharply in recent years in urban areas of developing countries—using behavioural methods may increase the probability of RTI/STI and HIV/AIDS. Although our survey finds that the incidence of RTI/STI is not significantly higher among current users of behavioural methods, compared to current users of male condoms, this possibility should not be overlooked.

This weakens the natural–technological dichotomy argument often cited in literature to justify reliance on behavioural contraception. Rather than building a romantic view of reliance on behavioural methods, one should recognize that while there is considerable discussion about real or imagined side effects of contraception pills, the dangers of using emergency pills are not so well known. This is why behavioural method users continue to rely on withdrawal and rhythm—despite unintended pregnancies or even failure to get sexual satisfaction—using emergency contraception pills as a backup.

In fact, analysis of gender parity and choice of contraceptive methods using NFHS data indicates that son preference has been the motivating factor underlying choice of contraceptive methods over the reproductive cycle. Initially, the urban elite may prefer less invasive contraceptive methods without side effects—even if they are less reliable. Once couples attain targeted family *size* and *composition*, greater weightage is assigned to reliability, with a shift to modern contraceptive methods.

Analysis of survey data presents somewhat different results. Examination of the relationship between parity and contraception use indicates that the use of behavioural methods is higher among couples with only one child. The use of modern reversible methods, however, steadily declines with number of living children, while couples with two or more children tend to adopt irreversible methods. If we consider gender of the living children, via the concept of gender parity, we get similar findings. Couples with one child—irrespective of gender—are more likely to use behavioural methods; if they have a higher parity—again irrespective of the gender—there appears to be a shift to irreversible contraception methods. Thus, (simple) parity, rather than *gender* parity, appears to be more important in determining contraception choice. This apparently vindicates that our research hypothesis was that women with unsatisfied fertility preferences (Husain et al. 2013) or ambiguous about pregnancy timings (Fisher 2000) will prefer to use behavioural methods; once their targeted fertility level is attained, they shift to modern methods, commonly perceived to be more reliable (Husain et al. 2013).

However, the presence of son preference revealed in the analysis of NFHS data is absent in the primary survey data. There may be two reasons for the variation in results.

(a) One is the differences in sample characteristics. The analysis of NFHS data had been carried out on a sample consisting of currently married women who had at least 12 years of schooling (that is, higher secondary passed). Further, almost all the respondents (barring 37, comprising 0.5 % of the sample in

West Bengal) were non-graduates. In contrast, the primary survey has targeted graduates. The difference in educational level of the two samples may also have attributed to the variation in results.

(b) The second factor may be different in time periods—the NFHS survey was undertaken seven years earlier, in 2005. Subsequently, there has been a major transformation in attitudes and way of life of urban society with the spread of Western ideals. This may have eroded son preference, never as strong as in North India, in Kolkata.

The failure of both modernism and son preference to explain reliance on behavioural contraception methods means that we have to look beyond them. Chapters 5 and 6 discard the traditional approach to studying contraception choice. In Chap. 5, we look at combinations of methods and examine how the combinations changes with time and parity. In Chap. 6, on the other hand, we examine how techno-economic conditions have created a risk society characterized by stress, uncertainty, and risk. We argue that it is necessary to examine how the nature of this risk society affects sexual relations, fertility plans, and methods to attain such plans. We suggest that stress in modern societies affects the incidence of sexual intercourse, while risk calls for focussed investment in quality of a limited number of children—so that limiting fertility becomes an important objective. Given the lack of privacy of couples, this leads couples to rely on contraception methods that are reliable, easy to use, and easy to discard. As male condoms and withdrawal satisfy these properties, women tend to rely on behavioural methods either solely, or in conjunction with condoms. Although behavioural methods are not perfectly reliable, backed up by emergency contraception methods, they can be effectively used to control fertility.

7.1.4 From Method to Method Mix

Chapter 4 points out that the focus on current contraception method overlooks the fact that users generally rely on a combination of methods or alternate between methods within a very short time. This implies that shifting the focus of analysis from a single method to the *methods* being used may open up an interesting avenue of research. Such an analysis is undertaken using the data from the primary survey.

The analysis of method mix reveals that behavioural methods are the most popular method, as found in the analysis of responses on current use. The mix of condom and behavioural method is also found to be popular among respondents. However, when examining the reliance on behavioural methods over the life cycle, the U-shaped curve reported by Goldberg and Toros (1994) and also found in our analysis based on currently used method is absent. Instead, we observe an inverse U-shaped curve. The incidence of use of non-coitus-dependent modern methods, both reversible and irreversible, is low after marriage. At subsequent stages, however, their use increases. In particular, sterilization rises sharply. An examination of the motives underlying choice of method mix reveals that ease of use is an important factor for users of behavioural methods. In case of women using behavioural methods in combination with either condoms or modern reversible methods, reliability is cited as motivating their choice.

Gribaldo et al. (2009) and Fisher (2000) had reported that women ambiguous about the timing of conception or seeking spontaneity in conception may use behavioural methods. This is not supported by our study. Users of behavioural methods, singly or in combination with other methods, are found to plan their pregnancies. Coupled with the short duration between marriage and first conception (about 78 % of women had conceived within 3 years of their marriage), this may reflect the emphasis on maternity in the life of an Indian woman and the social stigma still placed on sterility. However, when we investigated the relationship between choice of contraception mix and nature of pregnancy (whether planned or unplanned), we observed a high rate of failure among users of behavioural methods. This would indicate that unlike the Italian male, Indian men are far from being masters of their fertility.

An examination of the relationship between outcome of pregnancy and choice of contraception mix displays a shift to behavioural methods (singly or in combination with condoms) after a live birth. This may reflect the irregularity and reduced intensity of cohabitation, requiring a method that can be adopted at the time of intercourse. From the second conception onwards, particularly if it results in a live son, there is a shift towards modern methods. This evidence explains Basu's (2005) finding that users of modern methods have higher parity by indicating that it is women with higher parity who adopt modern contraception. Not that this is only an indication of a possible shift as we do not know what method the women were using before the conception.

7.2 Transition Matrices

The utility and formation of the transition matrix has been discussed in detail in Chap. 6. Although such matrices have not been used in the analysis of contraception decisions, they enable us to trace choice of contraception mix over conceptions. We find that after the first conception, there is an across the board shift to behavioural methods. After the second and third conceptions, there are shifts to behavioural methods—only users of behavioural methods (singly, or in combination with condoms) continue with the method being used earlier. Although use of non-coitus-dependent modern methods remains low, an increase in proportion using such methods may be observed, particularly from users of male condom (singly or in combination with behavioural methods).

Practical consideration underlies this transition. After marriage, when sexual pleasure is the dominant reason for cohabitation, sexual intercourse is spontaneous. Subsequently, when reproduction becomes the primary motive of cohabitation, intercourse transforms to a planned activity. Once children are born and marriage loses its novelty, the frequency of sexual intercourse declines and becomes irregular—partly because of work and family pressure, partly because children sleep with their parents. Cohabitation occurs in intervals snatched from the hustle and bustle of daily life, a result of manoeuvring to obtain privacy or during weekends and holidays. In such situations, methods such as contraceptive pills, IUDs, and other reversible non-coitus-dependent modern methods are not appropriate. More convenient are coitus-dependent methods, such as withdrawal or male condoms, and it is to these methods, or their combinations, that couples shift, keeping emergency contraceptive pills as a backup. At above replacement levels of parity, couples also shift to modern methods to ensure that further conceptions do not occur. In these cases, reliability dictates choice of contraception method mix. The increasing incidence of gynaecological problems (due to awareness, readiness to seek treatment, and better detection facilities) also leads to sterilization, eliminating the need for contraception, among women with one or more children.

7.3 Summing Up and the Road Ahead

To sum up, the findings of the report indicate that behavioural methods are a major means of regulating fertility among urban elite in India and in Kolkata. However, the dichotomy between users of modern methods and behavioural methods is questionable as couples use a combination of methods; further, this combination varies over the reproductive cycle of women, depending upon the outcome of earlier conceptions. Contraception choice is not a static choice, but has a dynamic component. The same woman may use different method, or method combinations, at different points of time so that classification of users becomes conceptually difficult and can lead to specification errors.

Before the first conception, a high proportion of users rely on behavioural methods; after the second conception, more women shift from modern to behavioural methods. At higher levels of parity, however, the use of non-coitus-dependent modern methods also starts increasing. The respondents of our survey have well-defined fertility plans and manage to regulate their parity, though not conceptions, as effectively. The failure rate of behavioural methods is compensated by reliance on emergency contraceptive pills. This is an undesirable trend in view of the side effects of emergency contraceptive pills. It is necessary to educate users about such side effects and regulate the use of emergency contraceptive pills.

Before concluding, we should note an important factor that has not been studied in this report. While explaining the fertility decline in Europe, Anderson (1986: 293) had argued that non-socio-economic variables such as religion, language, ethnicity, and region explain much of the variation in marital fertility decline. Our analysis indicates that the reliance on behavioural methods is particularly high in urban West Bengal.

While exploring NFHS data, we had also found that it was among the Bengali-speaking community—not only in West Bengal, but in all other states—that the use of withdrawal and rhythm was high. This needs further analysis. Obviously, there are factors beyond education, occupation, and standard of living that are at work here. But, there are dangers in constructing a sociological theory of fertility along Weberian lines, or in reviving the belief held by classical social anthropologists that there are national characteristics. Any such theory should not remain satisfied with explaining fertility in terms of norms and values; it must also explain the emergence of cultural norms and values (Andorka 1986; Hawthorn 1970). Such studies may cut across political boundaries, creating units based on language as a proxy for culture, out of the neighbouring countries of India and Bangladesh (Amin et al. 2002; Basu and Amin 2000).

It is also necessary to undertake cross-country comparisons focussing on countries exhibiting a high extent of reliance on traditional methods. We need to examine the common factors, if any, between users, whether differences in socio-economic factors contribute to varying levels of effectiveness, and the role of culture in contraceptive choice. Such refinements of the present study are left as a task for the future.

Finally, our study also questions the mainstream approach to contraception choice. In large-scale surveys on reproductive health, the focus is on current and ever use of contraception, with the implicit assumption that the respondent uses a single method at a point of time. Further, possible reasons for non-use of contraception methods are typically sought among the following explanations:

(i) *Not married*;
(ii) *Fertility related*: Infrequent or no sex, menopausal problem, subfecund, wants more children;
(iii) *Opposition to contraception use*: from respondent, partner, others, religious prohibitions, fatalistic attitude;
(iv) *Lack of knowledge*: Lack of awareness about either method or source; and
(v) *Method related*: Health concern, fear of side effects, lack of access, cost, inconvenient to use, interferes with body.

The discussion on fertility regulation in Chaps. 5 and 6, however, indicates that actual contraception choice is more complex. Women may use not a single method, but combination of methods. Even this combination may change over time. Further, the choice of method or their combinations is determined by factors determining frequency and timing of intercourse, such as the stress of living in a globalized risk society, occupation, working habits, and sleeping patterns. We argue that incorporating these issues in large-scale surveys on reproductive health is a major challenge that policy makers and researchers must face in the coming decades.

References

Amin, S., Basu, A. M., & Stephenson, R. (2002). Spatial variation in contraceptive use in Bangladesh: Looking beyond the borders. *Demography, 39*(2), 251–267.

Anderson, B. (1986). Regional and cultural factors in the decline of marital fertility in Western Europe. In A. J. Coale & S. C. Watkins (Eds.), *The decline of fertility in Europe*. Princeton NJ: Princeton University Press.

Andorka, R. (1986). The decline of fertility in Europe: Review symposium. *Population and Development Review, 12*(2), 329–334.

Basu, A. M. (2005). Ultramodern contraception: Social class and family planning in India. *Asian Population Studies, 1*(3), 303–323.

Basu, A. M., & Amin, S. (2000). Conditioning factors for fertility decline in Bengal: History, language identity, and openness to innovations. *Population and Development Review, 26*(4), 761–794.

Castiglioni, M., Dalla Zuanna, G., & Loghi, M. (2001). Planned and unplanned births and conceptions in Italy, 1970–1995. *European Journal of Population, 17*(3), 207–233.

Dalla Zuanna, G., De Rose, A., & Racioppi, F. (2005). Low fertility and limited diffusion of modern contraception in Italy during the second half of the twentieth century. *Journal of Population Research, 22*, 21–48.

Erfani, A., & Yuksel-Kaptanoglu, I. (2012). The use of withdrawal among birth limiters in Iran and Turkey. *Studies in Family Planning, 43*, 21–32.

Fisher, K. (2000). Uncertain aims and tacit negotiation: Birth control practices in Britain 1925–1950. *Population Development Review, 26*, 295–317.

Goldberg, H. I., & Toros, A. (1994). The use of traditional methods of contraception among Turkish couples. *Studies in Family Planning, 25*, 122–128.

Gray, A., Chowdhury, J. H., Caldwell, B., & Al-Sabir, A. (1997). *Traditional' family planning in Bangladesh*. Dhaka: Population Council.

Gribaldo, A., Judd, M. D., & Kertzer, D. I. (2009). An imperfect contraceptive society: Fertility and contraception in Italy. *Population Development Review, 35*, 551–584.

Hawthorn, G. (1970). *The sociology of fertility*. London: Collier-Macmillan.

Husain, Z., Ghosh, S., & Dutta, M. (2013). 'Ultramodern contraception' re-examined: Cultural dissent or son preference? *Asian Population Studies, 9*(3), 280–300.

Iyer, S. (2002). Religion and the decision to use contraception in India. *Journal for the Scientific Study of Religion, 41*(4), 711–722.

Jejeebhoy, S. J., & Xavier, A. J. F. (2012). *Injectable contraceptives: Perspectives and experiences of women and health care providers in India*. Population Council: New Delhi.

Johnson-Hanks, J. (2002). On the modernity of traditional contraception: Time and the social context of fertility. *Population and Development Review, 28*, 229–241.

Juarez, F., Cabigon, J., & Singh, S. (2009). High prevalence of traditional methods and unwanted pregnancies: Barriers to obtaining family planning services in the Philippines. *Paper presented in Population Association of America 2009 Annual Meeting, Detroit, Michigan, 30 April–2 May*. http://paa2009.princeton.edu/download.aspx?submissionId=90756. Accessed July 15, 2011.

Kovavisarach, E., & Saringcarnan, P. (2010). Coitus interruptus in female patients seeking services at Obstetrics and Gynecology Department in Rajavithi Hospital. *Journal of Medical Association Thailand, 93*, 1356–1359.

Nguyen, H. N., & Miller, P. (2012). The use of traditional contraceptive methods in a northern province in Vietnam. *Paper presented in Second Asian Population Conference, Bangkok, 26–29 August 2012*.

Rajaretnam, T., & Deshpande, R. V. (1994). Factors inhibiting the use of reversible contraceptive methods in rural South India. *Studies in Family Planning, 25*, 111–121.

Schneider, J., & Schneider, P. (1996). *Festival of the poor: Fertility decline and the ideology of class in Sicily 1860-1980*. Tucson: Arizona Press.

Sedgh, G., Hussain, R., Bankole, A., & Singh, S. (2007). *Women with an unmet need for contraception in developing countries and their reasons for not using a method, Occasional Report no. 37*. New York: Guttmacher Institute.

Sharma, S., & Pasha, A. (2011). Are muslim women behind in their knowledge and use of contraception in India? *Journal of Public Health and Epidemiology, 3*(13), 632–641.

Thapan, M. (1997). *Essays on gender and identity*. New Delhi: Oxford University Press.

Thapan, M. (2009). *Living the body: Embodiment, womanhood and identity in contemporary India*. New Delhi: Sage Publications.

Uberoi, P., & Bahadur, T. (2001). The woman's body in mid-life: Sociocultural and medical perspectives from South Asia. *Occasional Papers in Sociology*, No. 4, Institute of Economic Growth, New Delhi.

Appendix
Questionnaire

Indian Council of Social Science Research funded study undertaken by Economics Department, Presidency University on

"ULTRA-MODERN" CONTRACEPTION

As modern contraceptive methods have many side effects, women may be willing to use traditional contraceptive methods. The objective of this study is to examine the prevalence of traditional contraceptive method and the extent to which it is used successfully.

<table>
<tr><th colspan="2">Recruitment criteria</th></tr>
<tr><td>Currently married for at least 3 years</td><td>Yes</td></tr>
<tr><td>Divorced but not married for at least 5 years</td><td rowspan="3">If yes to all 3 then DROP</td></tr>
<tr><td>Does not have children</td></tr>
<tr><td>Not using contraceptive</td></tr>
<tr><td>Respondent is at least graduate</td><td>Yes</td></tr>
<tr><td>Husband is also at least graduate</td><td>Yes</td></tr>
<tr><td>Age is within 23-45 years</td><td>Yes</td></tr>
<tr><td>Resides in KMC / Bidhan Nagar</td><td>Yes</td></tr>
</table>

Informed consent

The questionnaire is being used to collect data on an ICSSR-funded study of frequency and usage patterns of traditional contraceptive methods.

Respondents are requested to cooperate with field investigators in filling in the questionnaire.

It will take about 25–30 min to complete the questionnaire. They should note the following points:

1. The purpose of the study is academic.
2. Participation in the survey is voluntary.
3. Respondents may withdraw from the interview at any stage.

Z. Husain and M. Dutta, *Fertility Control in a Risk Society*,
SpringerBriefs in Population Studies, DOI 10.1007/978-81-322-3685-6

4. Respondents may also refuse to answer any particular question.
5. Details of the respondent will be kept confidential.

QUESTIONNAIRE

	Respondent Code					
Time started		**Time ended**		**Date**		**Interviewer**
DEMOGRAPHIC PROFILE OF RESPONDENT						

1	Name (in block letters)	
Address:		
2	Land line	
3	Mobile	
4	Residential area	
5	Age (in completed years)	
6	Current marital status: Currently married 1; Widow 2; Divorcee 3; Separated 4; Other 9	
7	Age at first marriage	
8	Number of times married	
9	What is your religion? Hindu 1; Islam 2; Christian 3; Other 4; No Religion 5	
10	What is your caste? General 1; SC 2; ST 3; OBC 4; Not stated 5	
11	What language do you speak at home? Bengali 1; Hindi 2; Urdu 3; English 4; Others 5 Aapin baiRet ekan vaxaO kFa beln ? ba.la 1, ihi_d 2, Ud&u 3, l.erij 4, AnZ 5	
12	What is your education? Graduate 1; Post Graduate 2; Doctorate 3; PG Diploma/Certificate 4; Professional courses 5; Others 9	
13	Can you use the computer and internet? No 0; Only computer 1; Computer & internet 2	
14	Whether currently employed? No 0; Part-time (informal) 1; Part-time (formal) 2; Full-time 3	
15	What is your current occupation? Housewife 0; School teacher 1; College teacher 2; Clerk/Executive/Lower division Officer 3; Higher level Officer/Manager/Administration 4; Professional 5; Medical 6; Sales 7; Business 8, Others 9 (Specify)	
16	What is your husband's education? Graduate 1; Post Graduate 2; Doctorate 3; PG Diploma/Certificate 4; Professional courses 5; Others 9	
17	Whether husband is currently employed? No 0; Part-time (AS.giHt eqQ) 1; Part-time (S.giHt eqQ) 2; Full-time 3	
18	What is your husband's current occupation? Teacher 1; Clerk/Executive/Lower division Officer 2; Higher level Officer/Manager/Administration 3; Professional 4; Medical 5; Sales 6; Business 7; Others 9 (Specify)	
19	Number of living sons?	
20	Number of ever born sons?	
21	Number of living daughters?	
22	Number of ever born daughters?	
23	What is the family structure? Nuclear 1; With your in-laws 2; With your parents 3; Joint/Greater family 4	
24	What is your original residence? Kolkata 1; Within state 2; Mention state if outside West Bengal 3; Outside India 99	
STANDARD OF LIVING OF RESPONDENT		
25	Do you own LCD/LED TV/Home Theatre? No 0; Yes 1	
26	Do you own any mechanical water purifying system at home? No 0; Yes 1	
27	Do you own washing machine? No 0; Yes 1	
28	Do you own AC machine? No 0; Yes 1	
29	Do you own Car / 2-wheeler? No 0; 2-wheeler 1; non AC car 2; AC car 3	
30	Is your residence owned? No 0; Yes 1	
31	What is the super built space of your residence? Below 600 sq ft: 1; 601-1000 sq ft: 2; 1001-1500 sq ft: 3: 1500-3000 sq ft: 4; 3001 sq ft & above: 5; Other 9	
32	How much do you spend on domestic helps? (excluding driver) Nil 0; Rs.1-499 1; Rs.500–999 2; Rs.1000-1999 3; Rs.2000 & above 4	

33	Number of times you have gone abroad for a holiday in last five years?		
34	Number of times you have gone for a holiday outside state in 2010-12?		
35	Number of times you have gone for a holiday outside Kolkata in 2010-12? [Spent at least 2 nights]		
USE OF CONTRACEPTIVE METHODS :			
Are you aware of the following methods? No: 0; Yes: 1		Spontaneous	Aided
36	Male Condom		
37	Female Condom		
38	Pills		
39	Injectible/insertable		
40	IUD/Implants/Copper T/Multiload		
41	Foam / Jelly		
42	Female Sterilization		
43	Vasectomy / Male sterilization		
44	Withdrawal		
45	Rhythm / Calendar		
46	Have you/husband ever used any of the above methods? No: 0; Yes: 1		
47.a	What type of contraceptive are you using now? [If pregnant/sterilized, last method used] No method 0; Male Condom 1; Pill 2; IUD/Implant/Copper T 3; Injectible/insertable 4; Foam/Jelly 5; Withdrawal 6; Rhythm 7; Sterilization 8; Vasectomy 9; Other methods 10.		
48.b	Why have you chosen this method? NA 0; Easy to use 1; Reliable 2; Cheap 3; Comfortable 4; Doctor prescribed 5; Husband prefers 6; Fits in with religious convictions 7; Does not need much preparation 8; Other 9 **Up to two reasons**	1	
		2	
49.a	What method do **you** prefer most? No method 0; Condom 1; Pill 2; IUD/Implant/Copper T 3; Injectible/insertable 4; Foam/Jelly 5; Withdrawal 6; Rhythm 7; Sterilization 8; NA 9; Vasectomy 10; Other methods 11		
50.b	Why do you prefer this method? **Up to two reasons** NA 0; Easy to use 1; Reliable 2; Cheap 3; Comfortable 4; Doctor prescribed 5; Husband prefers 6; Fits in with religious convictions 7; Does not need much preparation 8; Other 9	1	
		2	
51.a	What method does **your husband** prefer most? No method 0; Condom 1; Pill 2; IUD/Implant/Copper T 3; Injectible/insertable 4; Foam/Jelly 5; Withdrawal 6; Rhythm 7; Sterilization 8; NA 9; Vasectomy 10; Other methods 11.		
51.b	Why does he prefer this method? **Up to two reasons** NA 0; Easy to use 1; Reliable 2; Cheap 3; Comfortable 4; Doctor prescribed 5; More satisfied 6; Fits in with religious convictions 7; Does not need much preparation 8; Don't know/Can't say 10; Other 9	1	
		2	
52	Who decides on which contraceptive method to use? NA 0; You 1; Jointly 2; Husband 3; Doctor 4; Jointly, with doctor's advise 5; Other 9		
53	Are you sterilized? No: 0; Yes: 1		
IF NO THEN SKIP TO Q NO. 60			
54	If you are sterilized: did you get sterilized immediately on delivering your last child? NA 0; No 1: Yes 2		
55	If there was a gap, how long (**in months**) was this gap?		
56	If there was a gap, why did you get sterilized? NA 0; Health problem 1; Doctor's advise 2; Husband wanted 3; Joint 4; You wanted 5; Others 9		
57	Who suggested sterilization? NA 0; Medical advise 1; Husband 2; Joint (on medical advise) 3; Joint (without medical advise) 4; Self 5; Others 9		
58	Do you regret being sterilized? NA 0; No 1; Yes 2		
TRADITIONAL CONTRACEPTIVES:			
59	Have you ever use withdrawal method? Never 0; Rarely 1; Sometimes 2; Frequently 3		

60	Did your husband discuss this method with you? No 0; Yes 1; NA 9		
61	Were you satisfied with this method? No 0; Yes 1; NA 9		
62	If not, why? **Up to two reasons.** NA 0; Not reliable 1; Did not satisfy you 2; Shameful 3; Husband failed to control himself 4; Not healthy 5; Others 9	1 2	
63	Have you ever use calendar/rhythm method? Never 0; Rarely 1; Sometimes 2; Frequently 3		
64	Did your husband discuss this method with you? No 0; Yes 1; NA 9		
65	Were you satisfied with this method? No 0; Yes 1; NA 9		
66	If not, why? **Up to two reasons** NA 0; Not reliable 1; Did not satisfy you 2; Shameful 3; Husband failed to control himself 4; Did not calculate safe period properly 5; Not healthy 6; Others 9	1 2	
67	Which of these two methods do you use more often? None 0; Rhythm 1; Withdrawal 2; Both 3		
68	Why do you use this method? **Give 2 reasons.**	1:	2:
NA 0; Reliable 1; Does not need prior preparation 2; No cost 3; Easy to use 4; Fits in with religious beliefs 5; Comfortable 6; Husband prefers 7; Leaves pregnancy to chance 8; Others 9			
69	Has rhythm method ever failed? No 0; Yes-did not do anything 1; Yes-Used medical abortion 2; Yes-Undertook MTP 3; DK/NA 9		
70	Has withdrawal method ever failed? No 0; Yes-did not do anything 1; Yes-Used emergency contraceptive 2, Yes- Undertook Medical abortion 3; Yes-Undertook MTP 4, DK/NA 9		
71	Do you know in which period of the month you are fertile? No: 0; Yes: 1		
72	In which period of the month are you fertile? During bleeding 1; Just after bleeding ends 2; 7-21 days after bleeding ends 3; Week before bleeding is due 4; Don't know 5		
73	Have you ever heard of emergency contraceptives? No 0; Yes 1		
74	Did you ever use emergency contraceptives? No 0; Yes 1; DK/NA 9.		
75.1	How many times did you get pregnant without prior planning? No 0; Yes 1		
75.2	Did you ever have to undertake a medical abortion? No 0; Yes 1; DK 9		
75.3	Did you tell husband that you were undertaking medical abortion? NA 0, No 1, Yes 2		
76	Did you ever have to undertake a MTP? No 0; Yes 1; DK 9		
77	Who decided on this? You 1; Jointly 2; Husband 3; Doctor insisted 4; Other 5; NA 9		
78	What is your ideal number of children? (Can be 0)		
79	What is your ideal number of sons? (Can be 0)		
80	What is your ideal number of daughters? (Can be 0)		
81	What is your husband's ideal number of children? (Can be 0; DK/can't say 9)		
82	What is your husband's ideal number of sons? (Can be 0; DK/can't say 9)		
83	What is your husband's ideal number of daughters? (Can be 0; DK/can't say 9)		
84	Have you ever had RTI/STI? No 0; Yes 1; DK/NA 9,		
85	Has your husband ever had RTI/STI? No 0; Yes 1; DK/NA 9		
EMPOWERMENT LEVEL OF RESPONDENT:			
Code: NA 0; Others 1; Husband 2; Joint 3; Respondent alone 4.			
86	Who has the final say on daily household purchases?		
87	Who has the final say on purchase of major household assets?		
88	Who has the final say on education of children?		
89	Who decides to take children to the doctor when they are ill?		
90	Who has the final say on choosing holiday destinations?		
91	Who has the final say on using contraceptives?		
CODE CHANGE			
92	Do you have a savings account which you operate yourself? No: 0; Yes: 1		
93	Do you have a say in deciding to purchase LIC policies? No: 0; Yes: 1		
94	Do you have a say in other financial investment? No: 0; Yes: 1		

95	If you reside in your owned house, in whose name is the house/flat? NA 0; In-laws 1; Husband (single/joint – not wife) 2; Joint with husband 3; In your parents name 4; In your name (single/joint – not husband) 5	
96	Do you belong to any society, club or (non-political) association? No: 0; Yes: 1	
97	Are you involved in the administration of such bodies? No: 0; Yes: 1	
98	Do you participate in any cultural activities? No: 0; Yes: 1	
99	Are you a member of any political party/political association? No: 0; Yes: 1	
100	Do you attend party/political association meetings regularly? No: 0; Yes: 1	
101	Are you an office bearer in the party/political association? No: 0; Yes: 1	
102	Do you take part in political processions, demonstrations, etc.? No: 0; Yes: 1	
103	Do you go to your husband's office parties? NA 0, Never 1, Sometimes 2, Generally 3, Always 4	
104	Do you go to your office parties alone? NA 0, I never go to parties 1; Husband always accompanies 2, Husband accompanies frequently 3; Husband accompanies occasionally 4; Husband never accompanies 5	
105	Do you go stay overnight (at least 4 times/annum) for office work? NA / No 0; Yes 1	
106	Do you go abroad (at least once last year) for office work? NA / No 0; Yes 1	
107	Do you think opposition of in-laws/husband is justified if the wife returns late from office due to work pressure/or works in a job involving night shift? Yes 1; Uncertain/Sometimes 2; Never 3	
108	Do you think opposition of in-laws/husband is justified if the wife returns late from office parties? Yes 1; Uncertain/Sometimes 2; Never 3	
109	Do you think that resentment of in-laws/husband is justified if the wife is unable to look after her children because of work pressure? Yes 1; Uncertain/Sometimes 2; Never 3	

Is respondent suitable for profiling? Yes/No
If yes, what is her preferred time? ________________

Use of contraceptive method over life cycle

How many times have you been pregnant? _______

Incident	Year of incident	Did you use any method?	Which method did you use mainly?	What is the main reason for using it?	Did you use traditional method?	Which method did you use?	What is the main reason for using it?	Nature of pregnancy	Outcome of
Marriage to pregnancy 1									
After pregnancy 1									
After pregnancy 2									
After pregnancy 3									
After pregnancy 4									
After pregnancy 5									
Last pregnancy to current									

Use any method: Never 0; Rarely 1; Frequently 2; Almost always 3; Always 4.

Main Method: No method 0; Male condom 1; Pill 2; IUD/copper T 3; Injectable/insertable 4; Foam/jelly 5; Withdrawal 6; Rhythm 7; Sterilization 8; NA 9; Vasectomy 10, Others 11

Reason: NA 0; Easy to use 1; Reliable 2; Cheap 3; Comfortable 4; Doctor prescribed 5; Husband prefers 6; Fits in with religious convictions 7; Does not need much preparation 8; Other 9

Traditional Method: Not used 0; Rarely used 1; Used often, but not main method 2; Main method 3.

Which method: NA 0; Withdrawal 1; Rhythm 2; Both 3

Reason: NA 0; Easy to use 1; Reliable 2; Cheap 3; Comfortable 4; Doctor prescribed 5; Husband prefers 6; Fits in with religious convictions 7; Does not need much preparation 8; Other 9

Nature of pregnancy: Planned pregnancy 1; Undecided 2; Did not want pregnancy at that time 3; NA 9

Outcome: Medical abortion 1; MTP (within 12 weeks) 2; MTP (after 12 weeks) 3; Miscarriage/still birth 4; Dead son: 5; Dead girl: 6; Live son: 7; Live girl: 8; NA 9, Twins 10.

MIX
Papier aus verantwortungsvollen Quellen
Paper from responsible sources
FSC® C105338

If you have any concerns about our products,
you can contact us on
ProductSafety@springernature.com

In case Publisher is established outside the EU,
the EU authorized representative is:
Springer Nature Customer Service Center GmbH
Europaplatz 3, 69115 Heidelberg, Germany

Printed by Libri Plureos GmbH
in Hamburg, Germany